4 WEEKS

Rebecca & Lucie

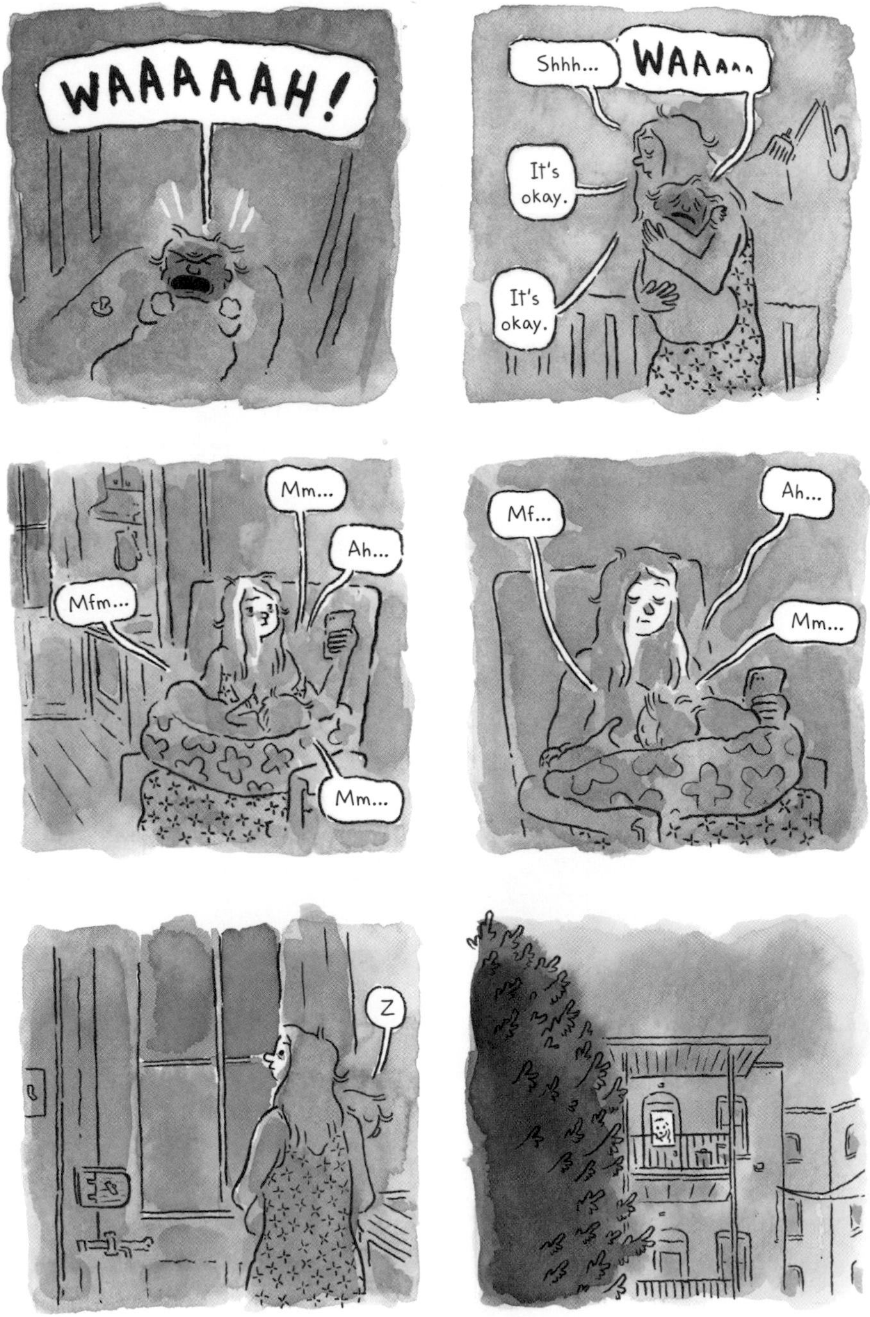
WAAAAAH!
Shhh...
WAAAAA
It's okay.
It's okay.
Mm...
Ah...
Mfm...
Mm...
Mf...
Ah...
Mm...
Z

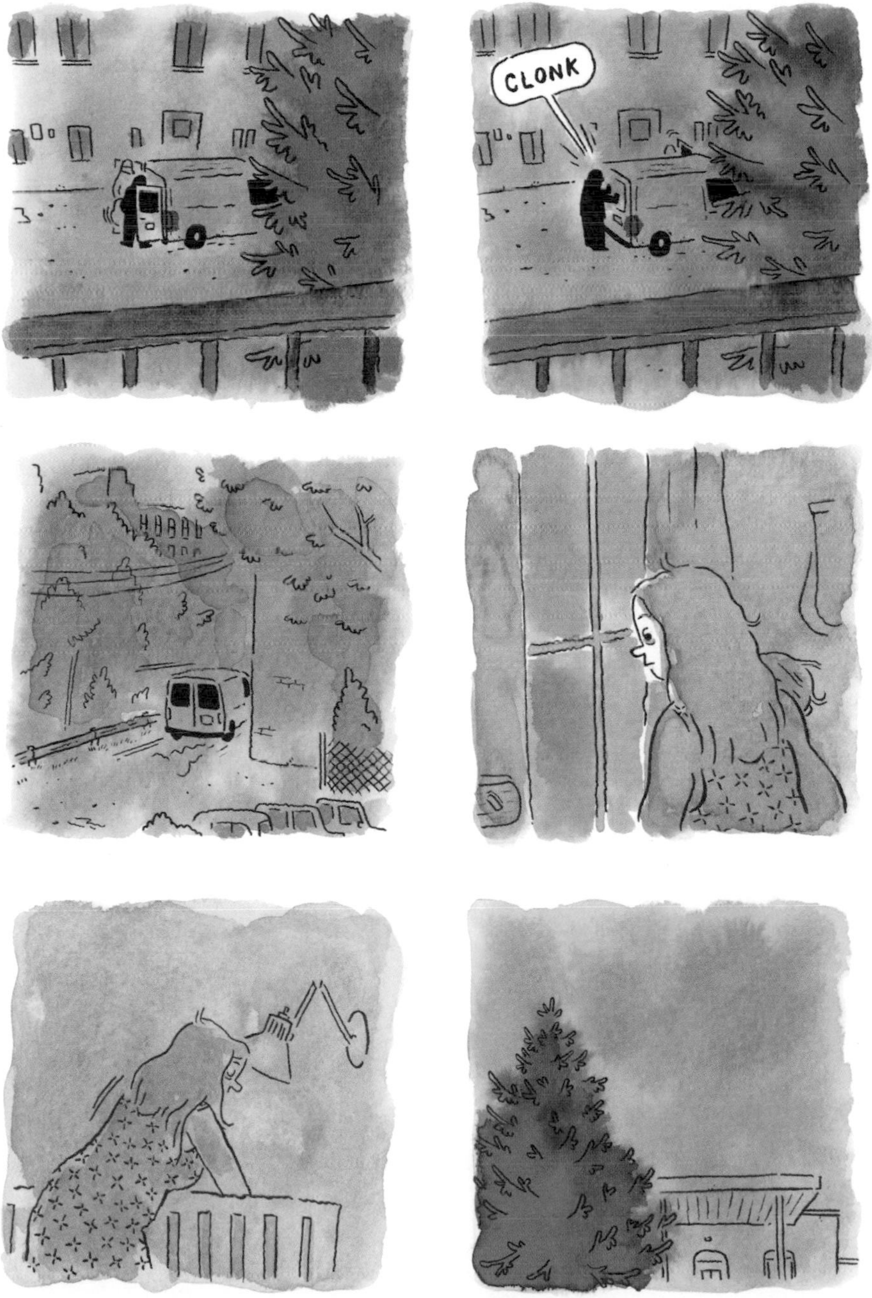
CLONK

The events depicted in this book are fiction, with the exception of pages 31–33, which were written with the help of Rebecca Lloyd.

drawnandquarterly.com
pascalgirard.com

ISBN 978-1-77046-464-3
First edition: June 2021
Printed in China
10 9 8 7 6 5 4 3 2 1

Cataloguing data available from Library and Archives Canada.

Published in the USA by Drawn & Quarterly, a client publisher of Farrar, Straus and Giroux. Published in Canada by Drawn & Quarterly, a client publisher of Raincoast Books. Published in the United Kingdom by Drawn & Quarterly, a client publisher of Publishers Group UK.

Pascal Girard acknowledges the financial support of the Canada Council for the Arts during the making of this book.

Drawn & Quarterly acknowledges the support of the Government of Canada and the Canada Council for the Arts for our publishing program, and the National Translation Program for Book Publishing, an initiative of the Roadmap for Canada's Official Languages 2013–2021: Education, Immigration, Communities, for our translation activities.

Canada

Drawn & Quarterly reconnaît l'aide financière du gouvernement du Québec par l'entremise de la Société de développement des entreprises culturelles (SODEC) pour nos activités d'édition. Gouvernement du Québec—Programme de crédit d'impôt pour l'édition de livres—Gestion SODEC.

Pascal Girard

Rebecca & Lucie
in the case of the missing neighbor

translated by Aleshia Jensen

Drawn & Quarterly

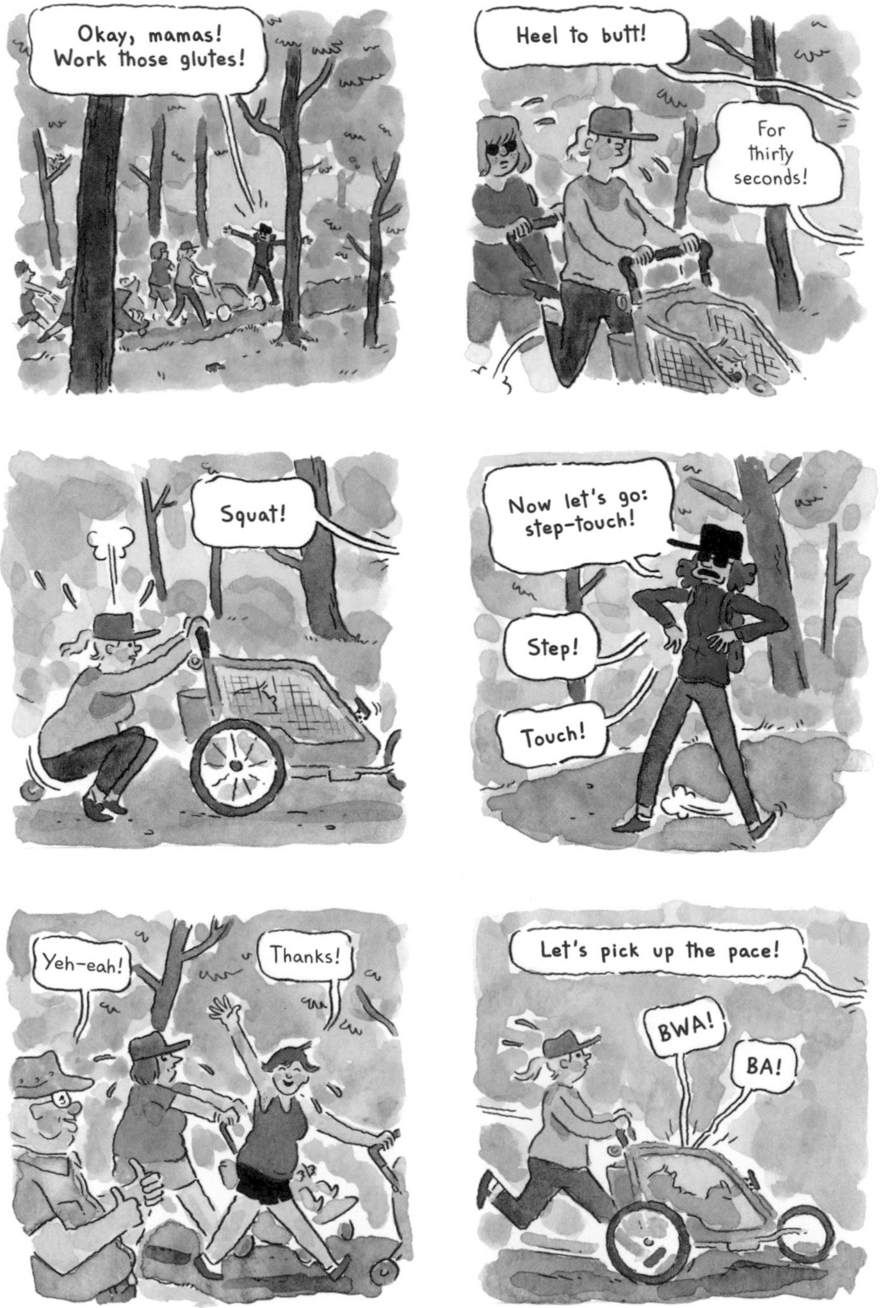
Okay, mamas! Work those glutes!
Heel to butt!
For thirty seconds!
Squat!
Now let's go: step-touch!
Step!
Touch!
Yeh-eah!
Thanks!
Let's pick up the pace!
BWA!
BA!

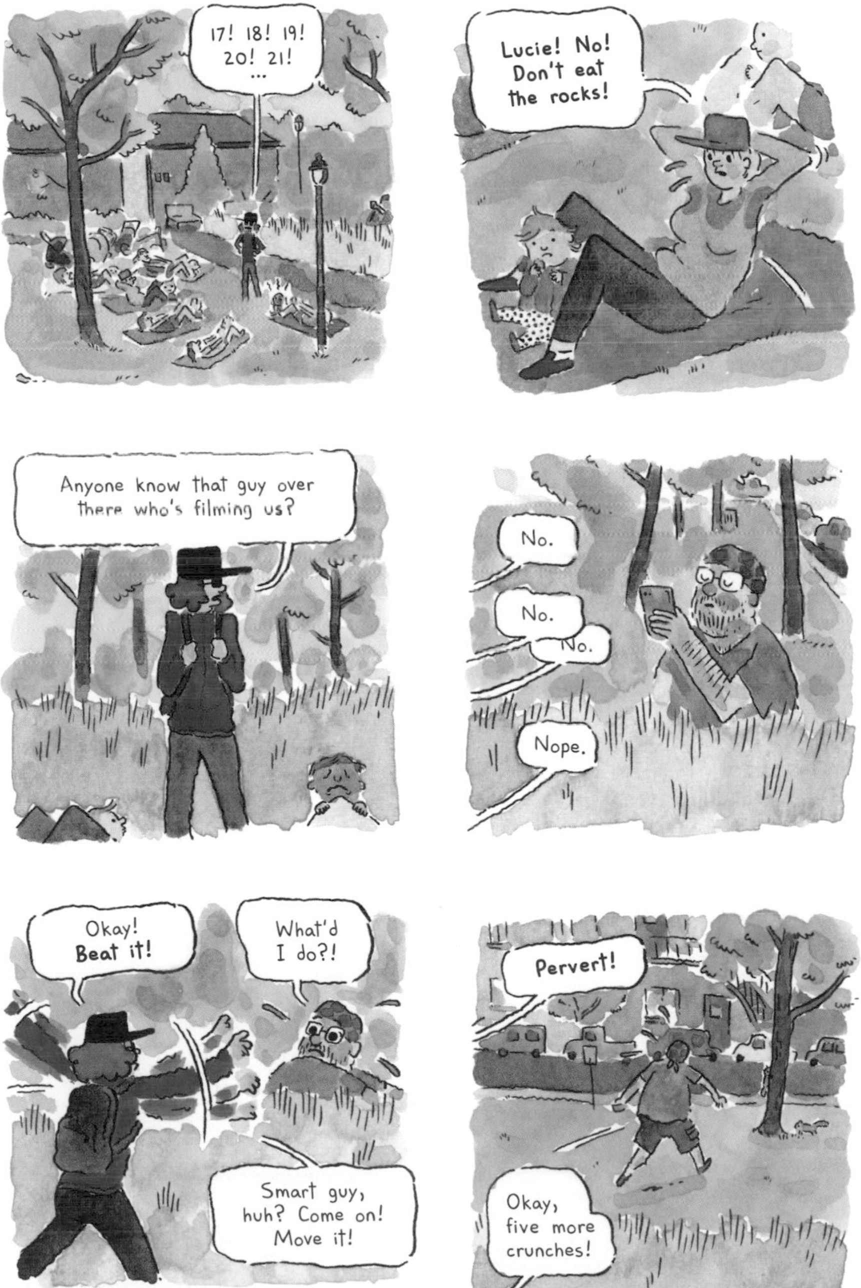
17! 18! 19! 20! 21! ...
Lucie! No! Don't eat the rocks!
Anyone know that guy over there who's filming us?
No.
No.
No.
Nope.
Okay! **Beat it!**
What'd I do?!
Smart guy, huh? Come on! Move it!
Pervert!
Okay, five more crunches!

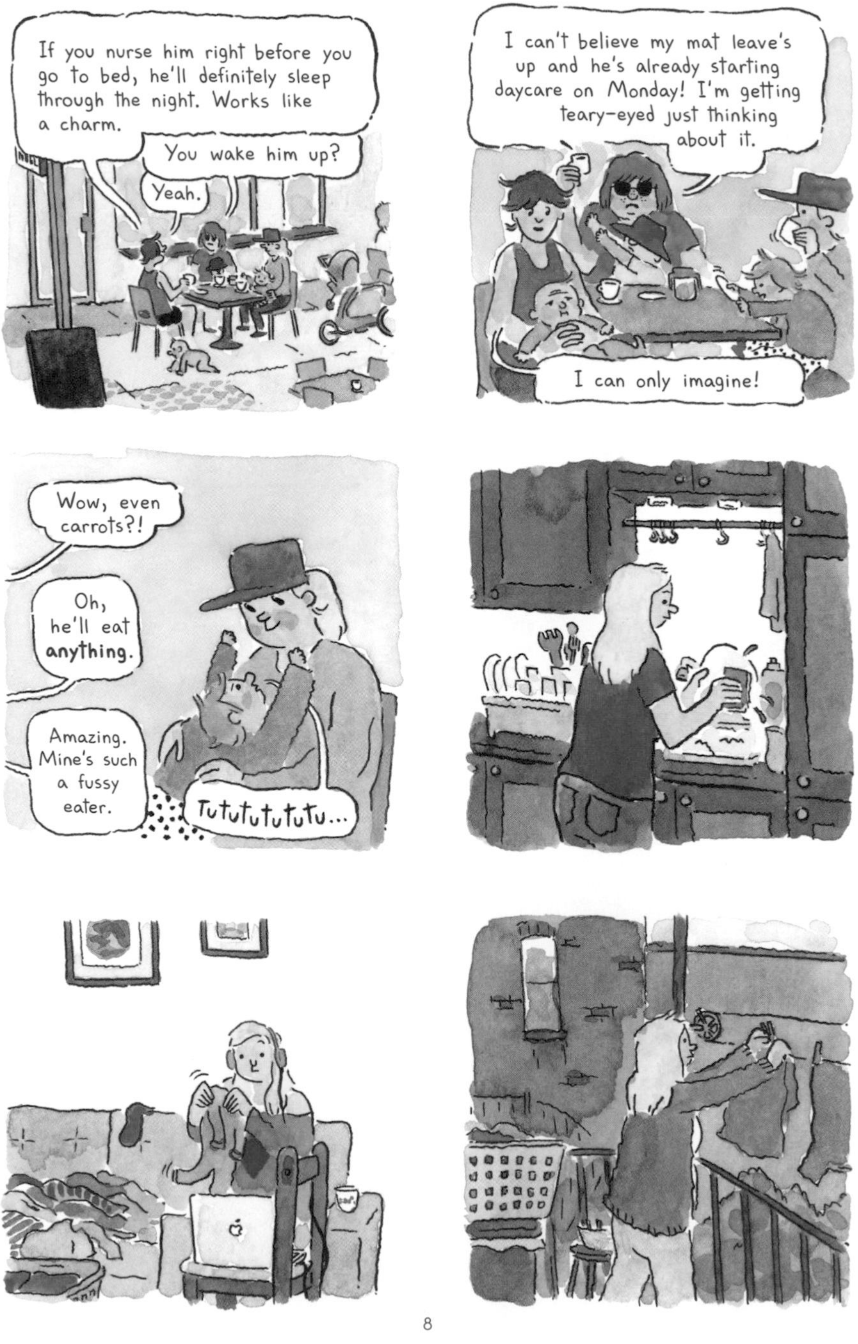
If you nurse him right before you go to bed, he'll definitely sleep through the night. Works like a charm.
You wake him up?
Yeah.
I can't believe my mat leave's up and he's already starting daycare on Monday! I'm getting teary-eyed just thinking about it.
I can only imagine!
Wow, even carrots?!
Oh, he'll eat **anything**.
Amazing. Mine's such a fussy eater.
Tutututututu...

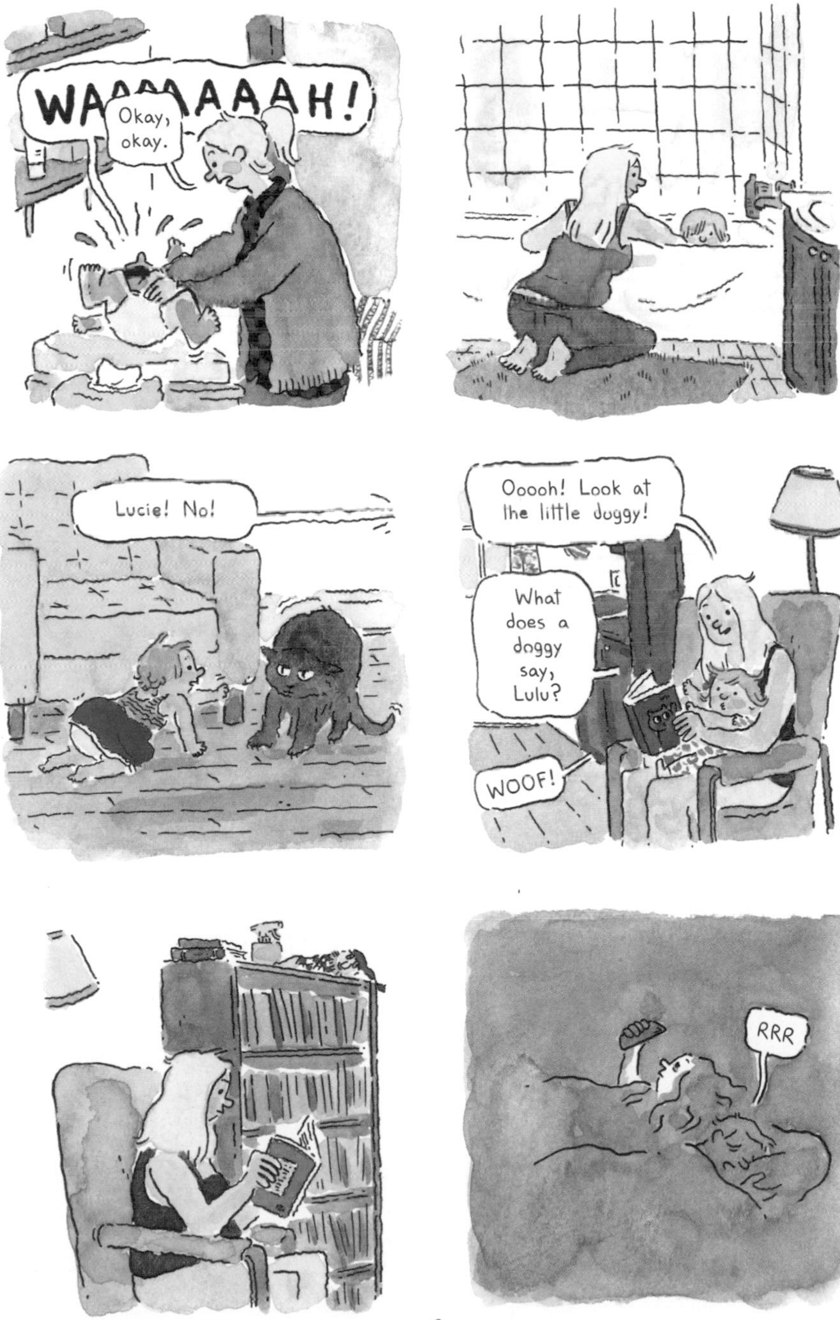
WAAAAAAAH!
Okay, okay.
Lucie! No!
Ooooh! Look at the little doggy!
What does a doggy say, Lulu?
WOOF!
RRR

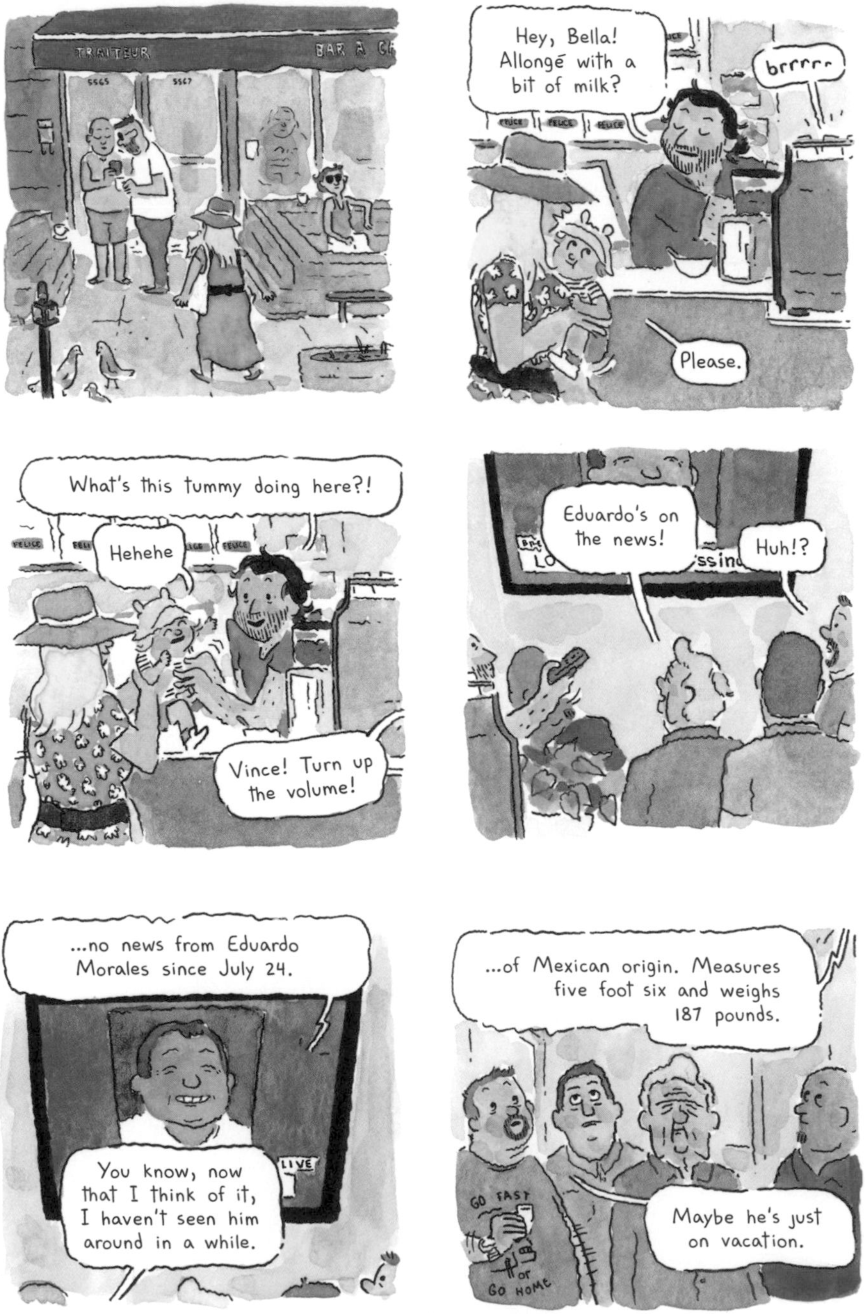
TRAITEUR
5565
5567
Hey, Bella! Allongé with a bit of milk?
brrrrr
Please.
What's this tummy doing here?!
Hehehe
Vince! Turn up the volume!
Eduardo's on the news!
Huh!?
...no news from Eduardo Morales since July 24.
LIVE
You know, now that I think of it, I haven't seen him around in a while.
...of Mexican origin. Measures five foot six and weighs 187 pounds.
GO FAST OR GO HOME
Maybe he's just on vacation.

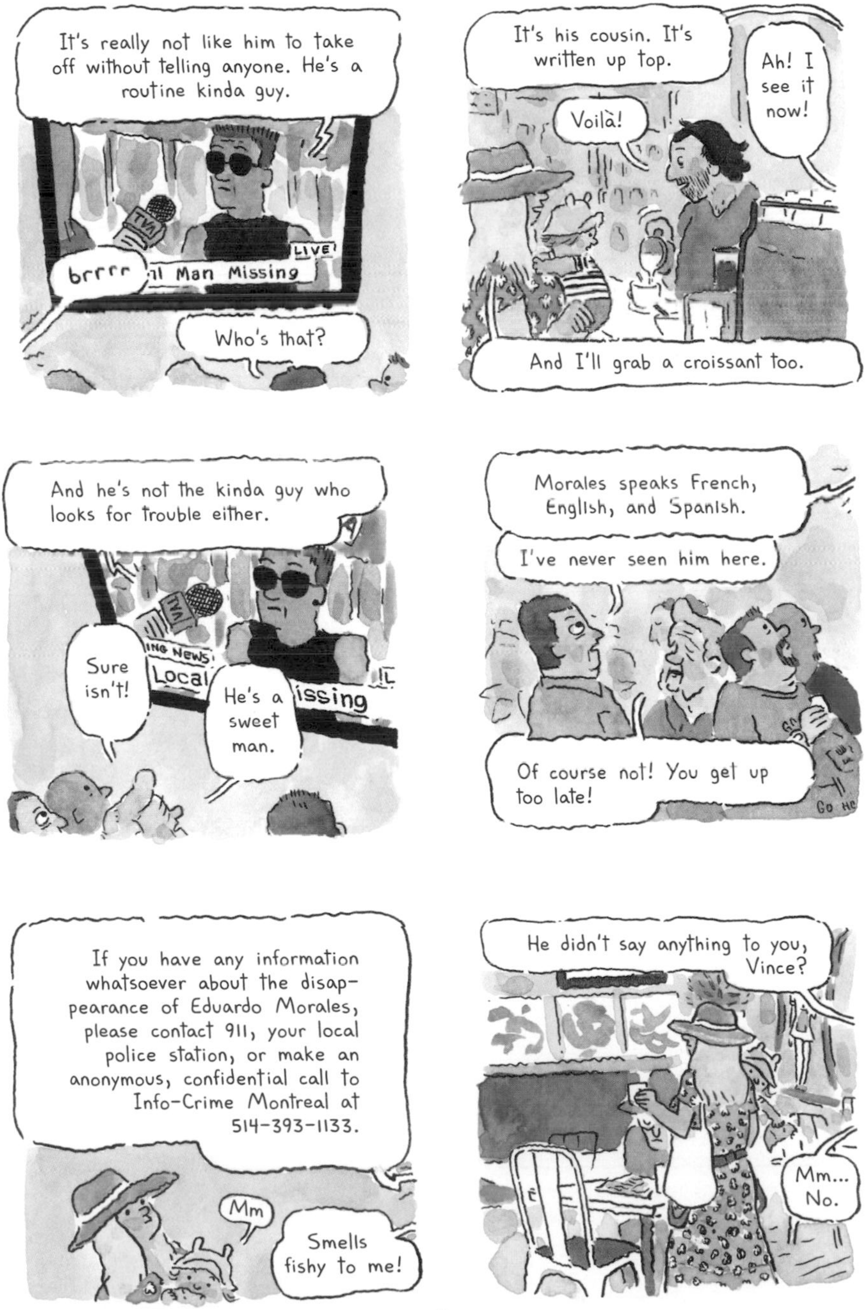
It's really not like him to take off without telling anyone. He's a routine kinda guy.
LIVE
brrrr
Man Missing
Who's that?
It's his cousin. It's written up top.
Ah! I see it now!
Voilà!
And I'll grab a croissant too.
And he's not the kinda guy who looks for trouble either.
Sure isn't!
ING NEWS
Local
issing
He's a sweet man.
Morales speaks French, English, and Spanish.
I've never seen him here.
Of course not! You get up too late!
GO HE
If you have any information whatsoever about the disappearance of Eduardo Morales, please contact 911, your local police station, or make an anonymous, confidential call to Info-Crime Montreal at 514-393-1133.
Mm
Smells fishy to me!
He didn't say anything to you, Vince?
Mm... No.

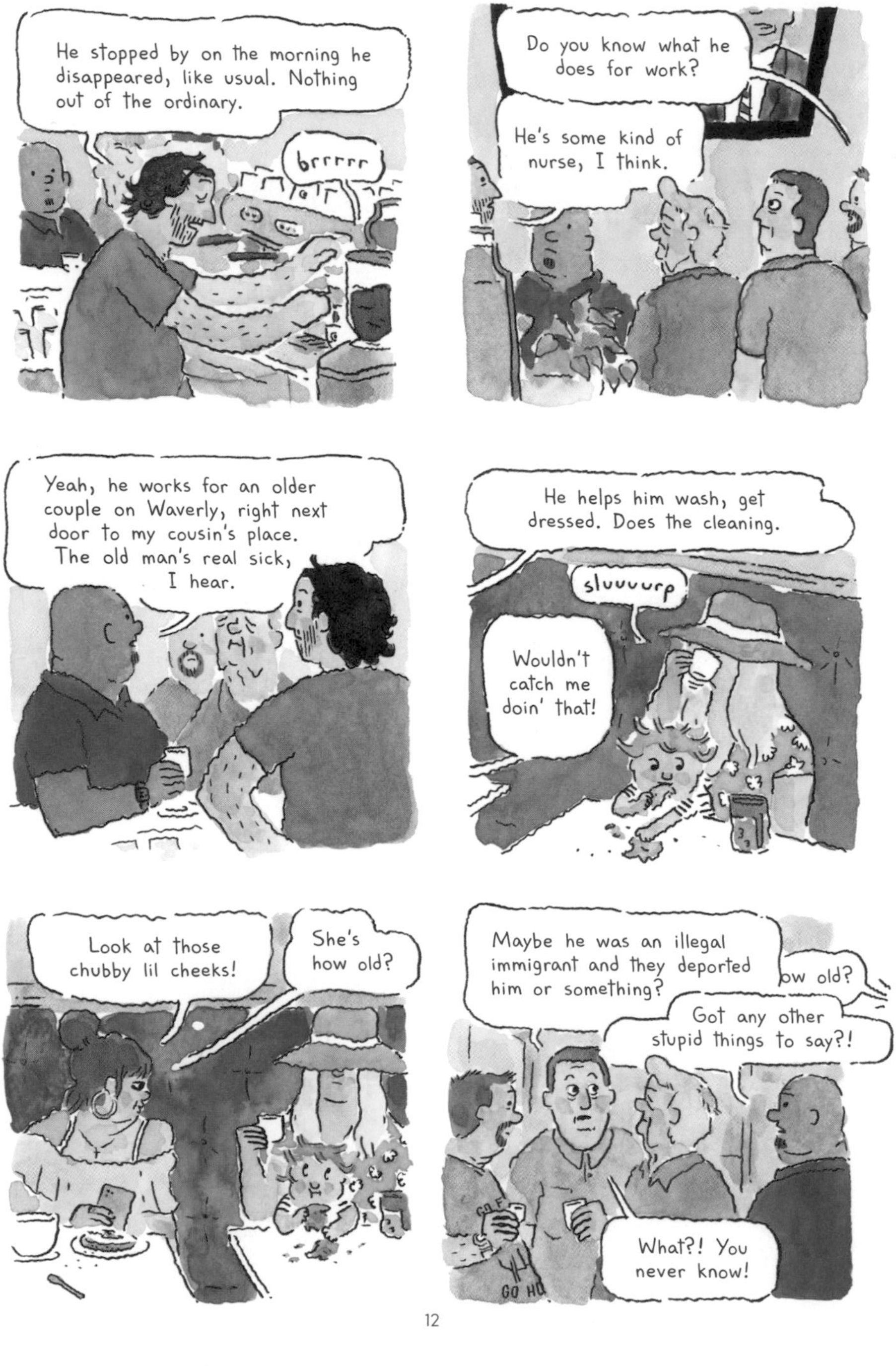
He stopped by on the morning he disappeared, like usual. Nothing out of the ordinary.
brrrrr
Do you know what he does for work?
He's some kind of nurse, I think.
Yeah, he works for an older couple on Waverly, right next door to my cousin's place. The old man's real sick, I hear.
He helps him wash, get dressed. Does the cleaning.
sluuuurp
Wouldn't catch me doin' that!
Look at those chubby lil cheeks!
She's how old?
Maybe he was an illegal immigrant and they deported him or something?
ow old?
Got any other stupid things to say?!
What?! You never know!

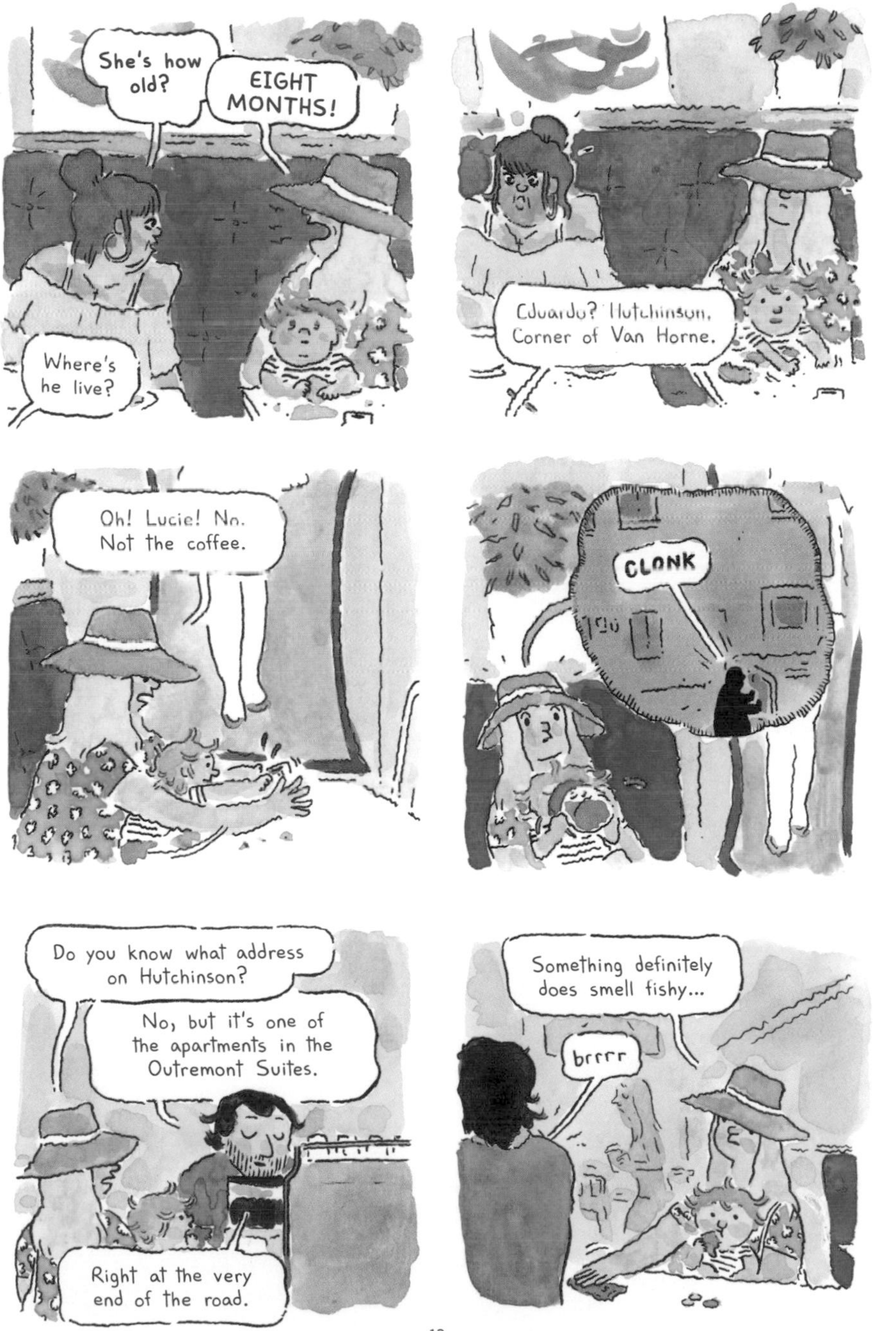
She's how old?
EIGHT MONTHS!
Where's he live?
Eduardo? Hutchinson, Corner of Van Horne.
Oh! Lucie! No. Not the coffee.
CLONK
Do you know what address on Hutchinson?
No, but it's one of the apartments in the Outremont Suites.
Right at the very end of the road.
Something definitely does smell fishy...
brrrr

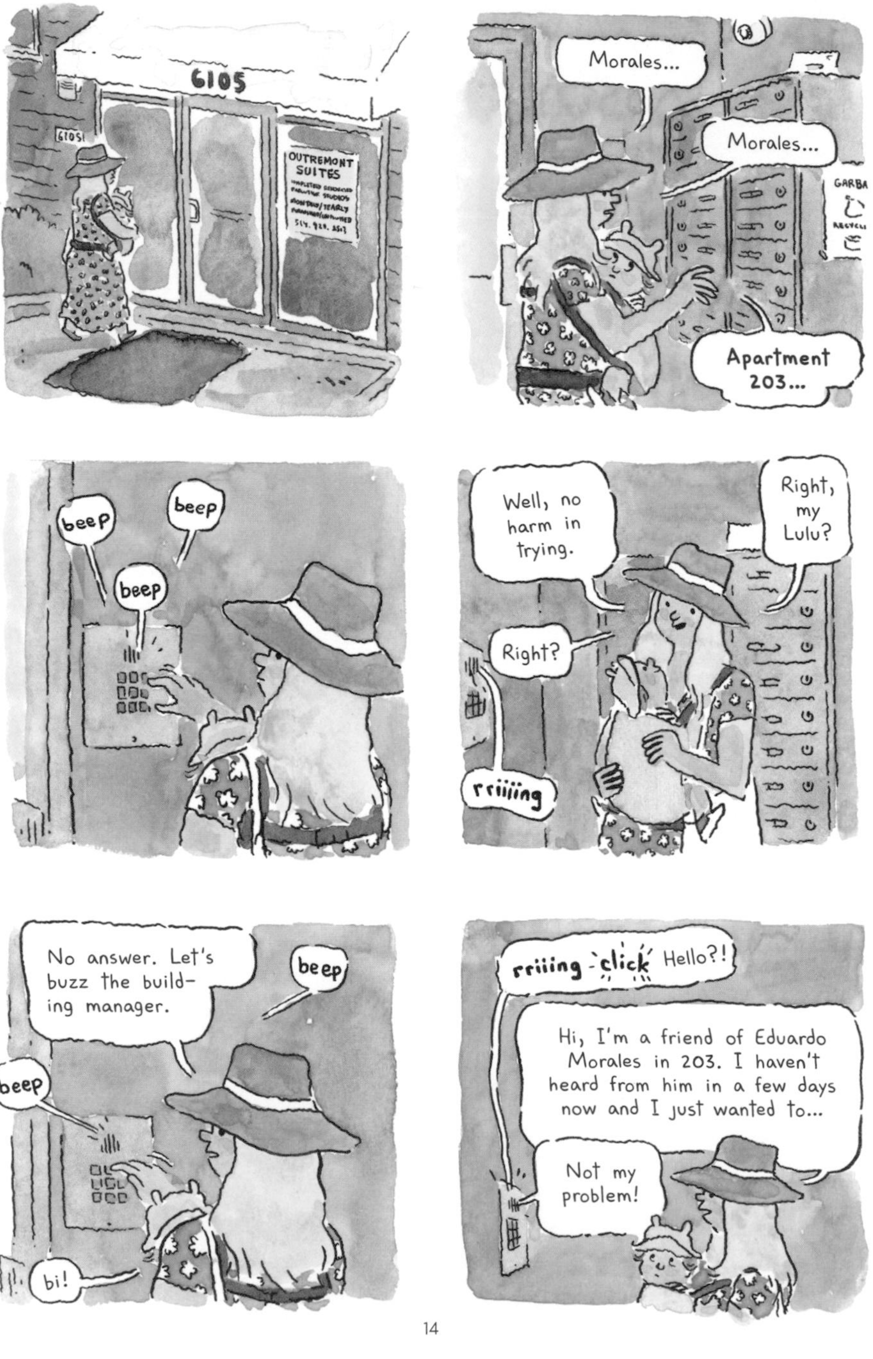
6105
6105
OUTREMONT SUITES
Morales...
Morales...
Apartment 203...
beep
beep
beep
Well, no harm in trying.
Right, my Lulu?
Right?
rriiiing
No answer. Let's buzz the building manager.
beep
beep
bi!
rriiing - click Hello?!
Hi, I'm a friend of Eduardo Morales in 203. I haven't heard from him in a few days now and I just wanted to...
Not my problem!

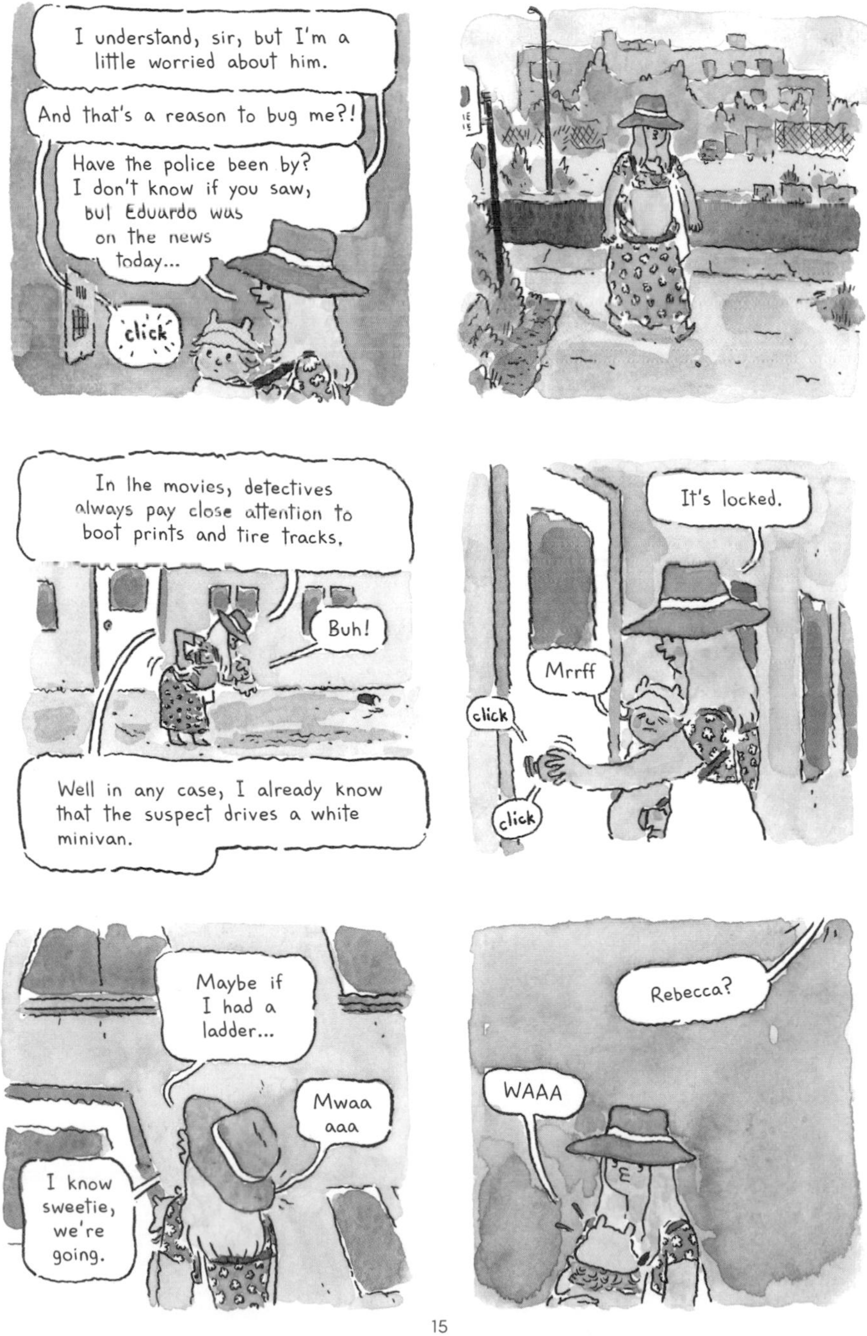
I understand, sir, but I'm a little worried about him.
And that's a reason to bug me?!
Have the police been by? I don't know if you saw, but Eduardo was on the news today...
click
In the movies, detectives always pay close attention to boot prints and tire tracks.
Buh!
Well in any case, I already know that the suspect drives a white minivan.
It's locked.
Mrrff
click
click
Maybe if I had a ladder...
Mwaa aaa
I know sweetie, we're going.
Rebecca?
WAAA

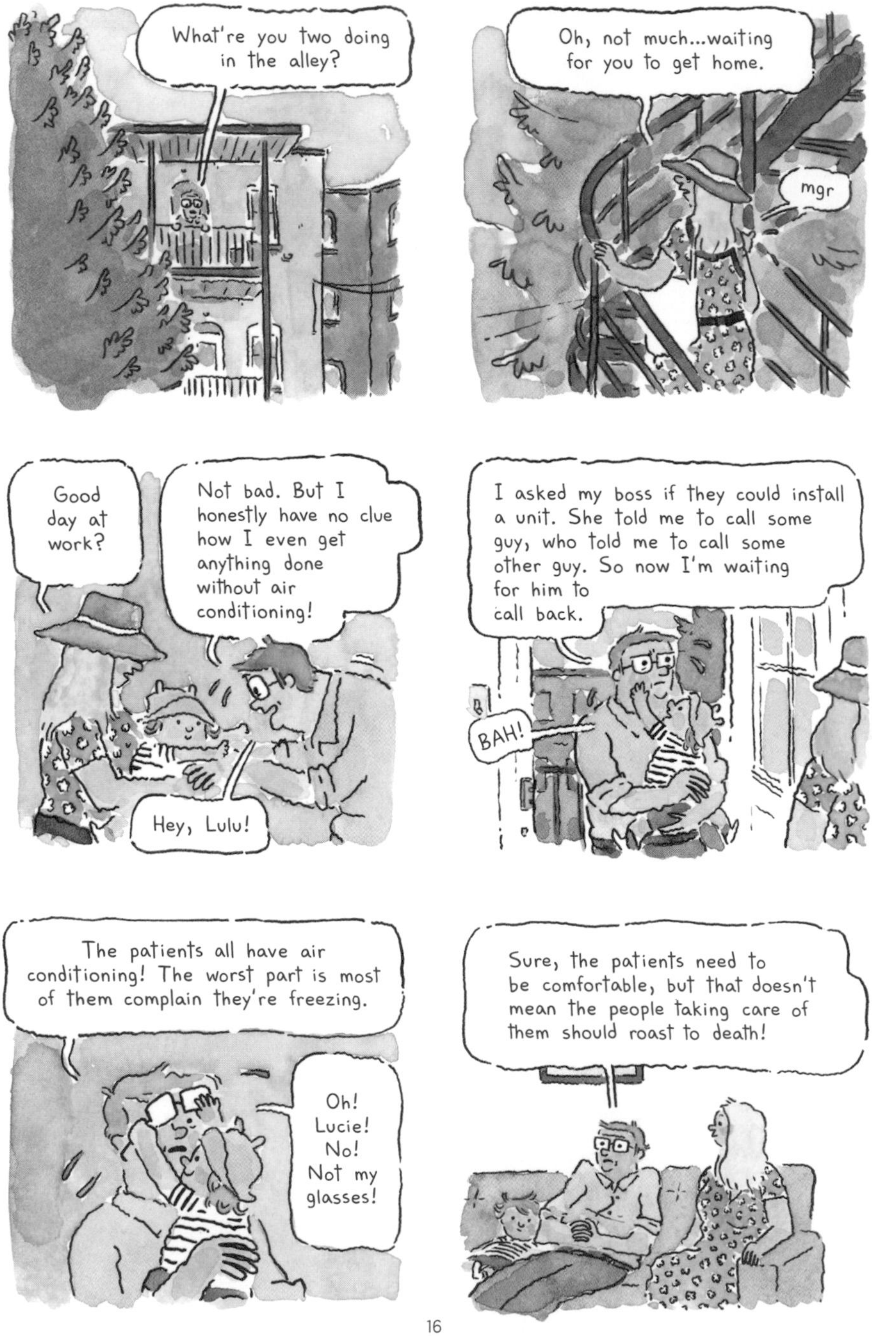
What're you two doing in the alley?
Oh, not much...waiting for you to get home.
mgr
Good day at work?
Not bad. But I honestly have no clue how I even get anything done without air conditioning!
Hey, Lulu!
I asked my boss if they could install a unit. She told me to call some guy, who told me to call some other guy. So now I'm waiting for him to call back.
BAH!
The patients all have air conditioning! The worst part is most of them complain they're freezing.
Oh! Lucie! No! Not my glasses!
Sure, the patients need to be comfortable, but that doesn't mean the people taking care of them should roast to death!

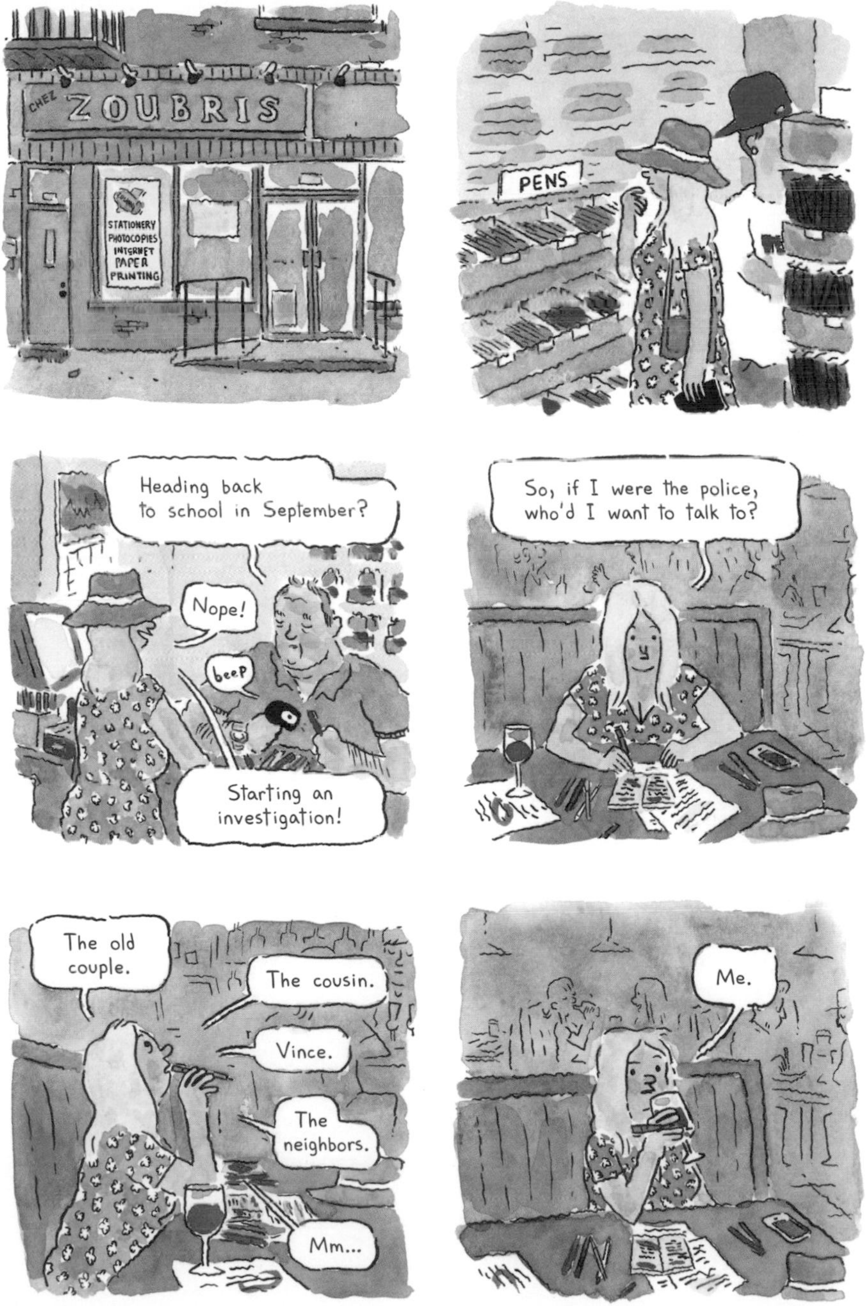
CHEZ
ZOUBRIS
STATIONERY
PHOTOCOPIES
INTERNET
PAPER
PRINTING
PENS
Heading back to school in September?
Nope!
beep
Starting an investigation!
So, if I were the police, who'd I want to talk to?
The old couple.
The cousin.
Vince.
The neighbors.
Mm...
Me.

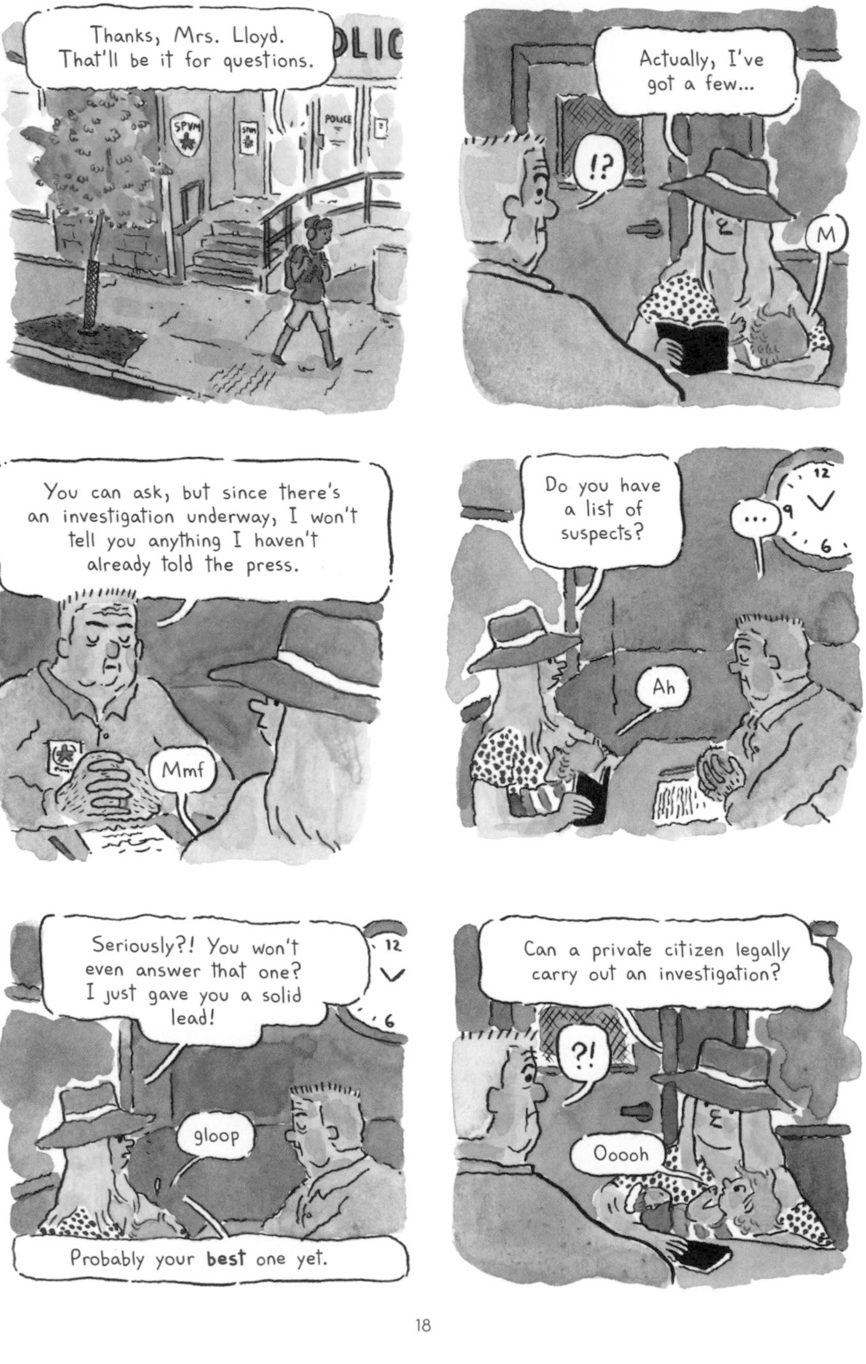
Thanks, Mrs. Lloyd. That'll be it for questions.
POLIC
SPVM
POLICE
Actually, I've got a few...
!?
M
You can ask, but since there's an investigation underway, I won't tell you anything I haven't already told the press.
Mmf
Do you have a list of suspects?
...
Ah
Seriously?! You won't even answer that one? I just gave you a solid lead!
gloop
Probably your **best** one yet.
Can a private citizen legally carry out an investigation?
?!
Ooooh

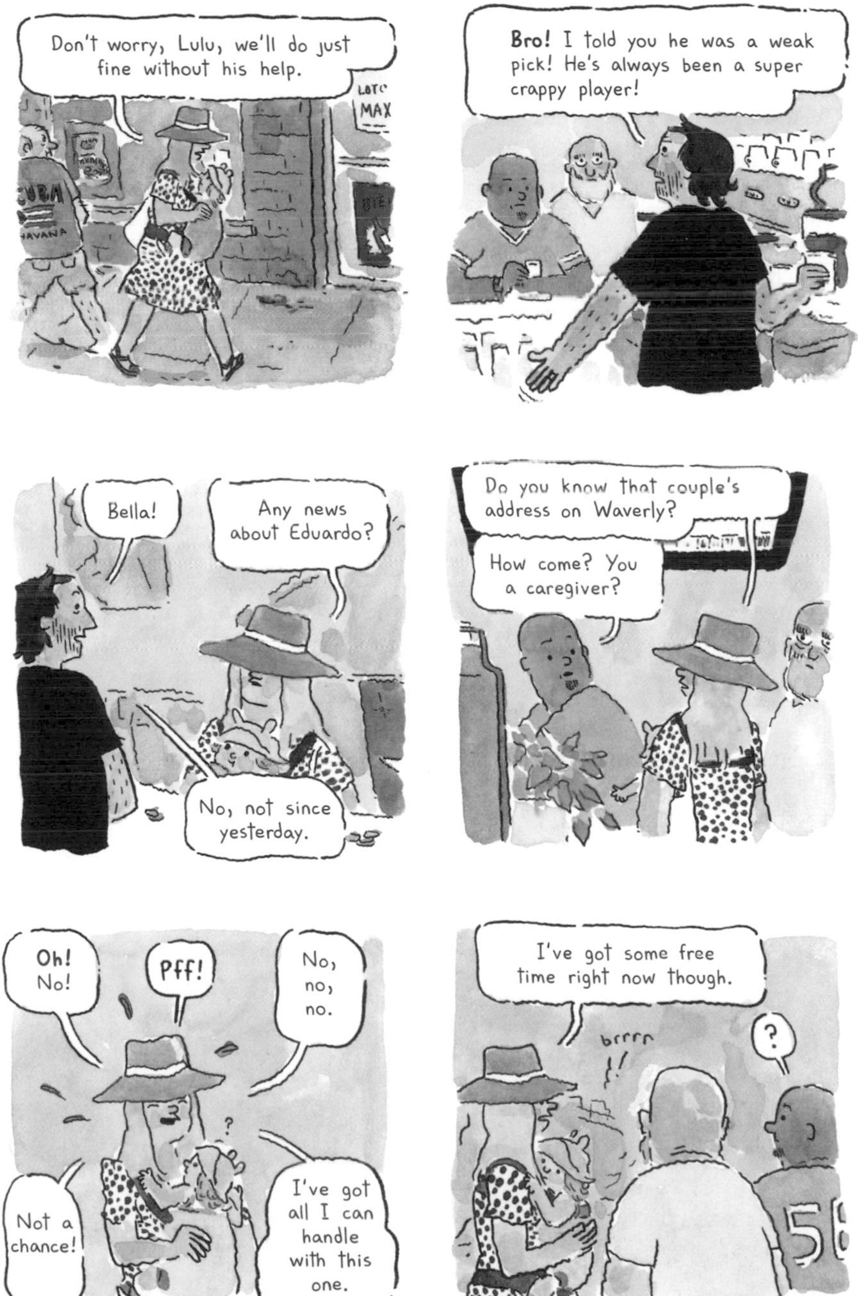
Don't worry, Lulu, we'll do just fine without his help.
LOTO
MAX
CUBA
HAVANA
Bro! I told you he was a weak pick! He's always been a super crappy player!
Bella!
Any news about Eduardo?
No, not since yesterday.
Do you know that couple's address on Waverly?
How come? You a caregiver?
Oh! No!
Pff!
No, no, no.
Not a chance!
I've got all I can handle with this one.
I've got some free time right now though.
brrrr
?
56

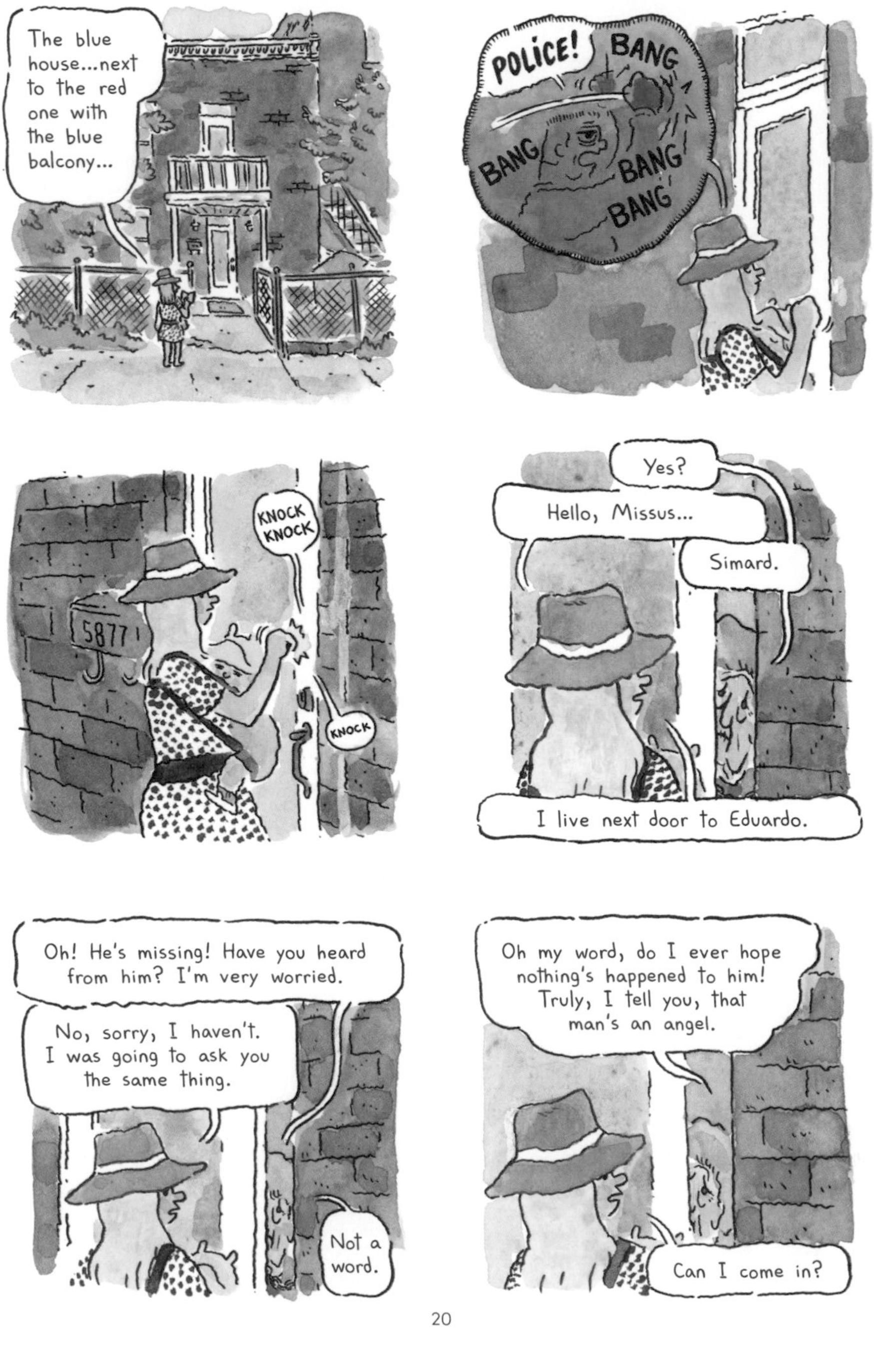

The blue house...next to the red one with the blue balcony...
POLICE!
BANG
BANG
BANG
BANG
KNOCK KNOCK
KNOCK
Yes?
Hello, Missus...
Simard.
I live next door to Eduardo.
Oh! He's missing! Have you heard from him? I'm very worried.
No, sorry, I haven't. I was going to ask you the same thing.
Not a word.
Oh my word, do I ever hope nothing's happened to him! Truly, I tell you, that man's an angel.
Can I come in?

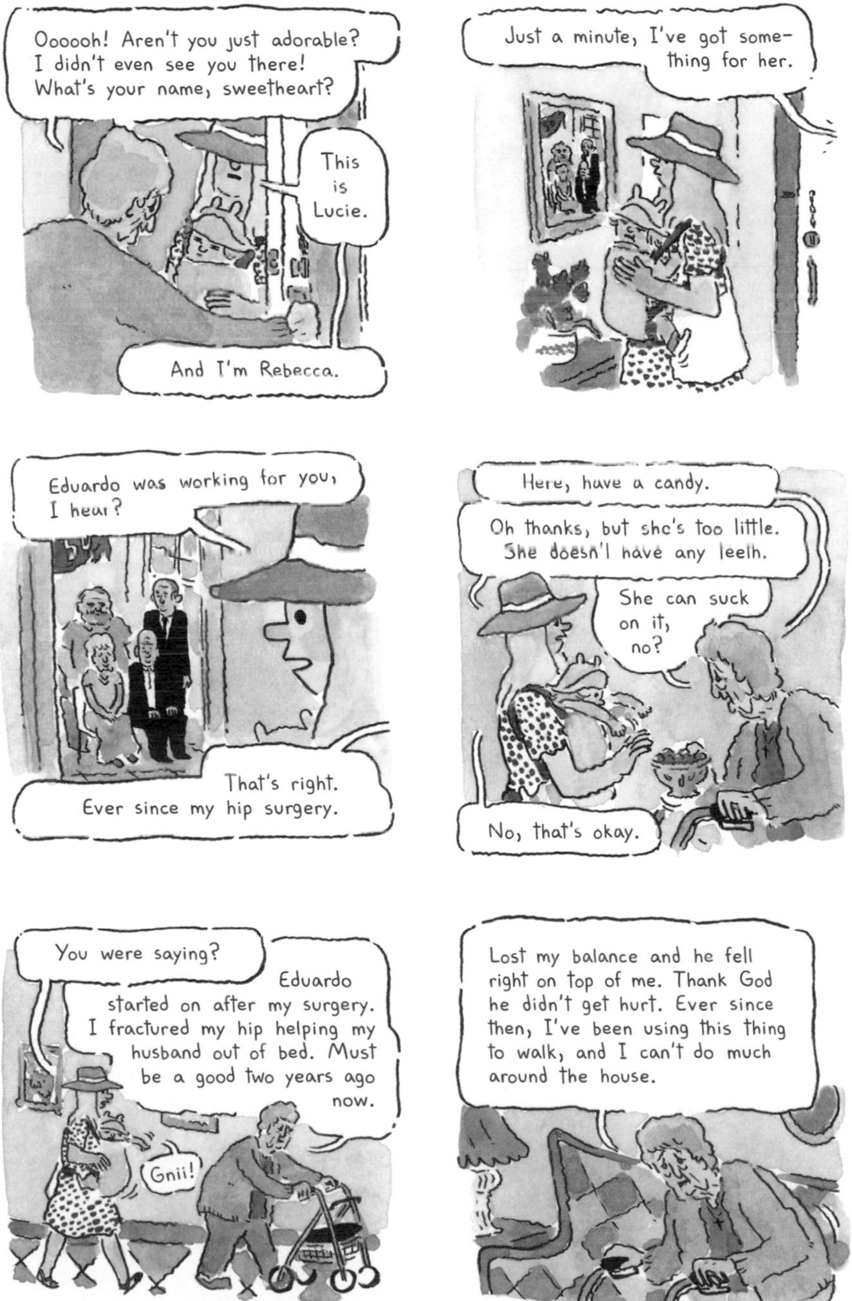
Oooooh! Aren't you just adorable? I didn't even see you there! What's your name, sweetheart?
This is Lucie.
And I'm Rebecca.
Just a minute, I've got something for her.
Eduardo was working for you, I hear?
That's right. Ever since my hip surgery.
Here, have a candy.
Oh thanks, but she's too little. She doesn't have any teeth.
She can suck on it, no?
No, that's okay.
You were saying?
Eduardo started on after my surgery. I fractured my hip helping my husband out of bed. Must be a good two years ago now.
Gnii!
Lost my balance and he fell right on top of me. Thank God he didn't get hurt. Ever since then, I've been using this thing to walk, and I can't do much around the house.

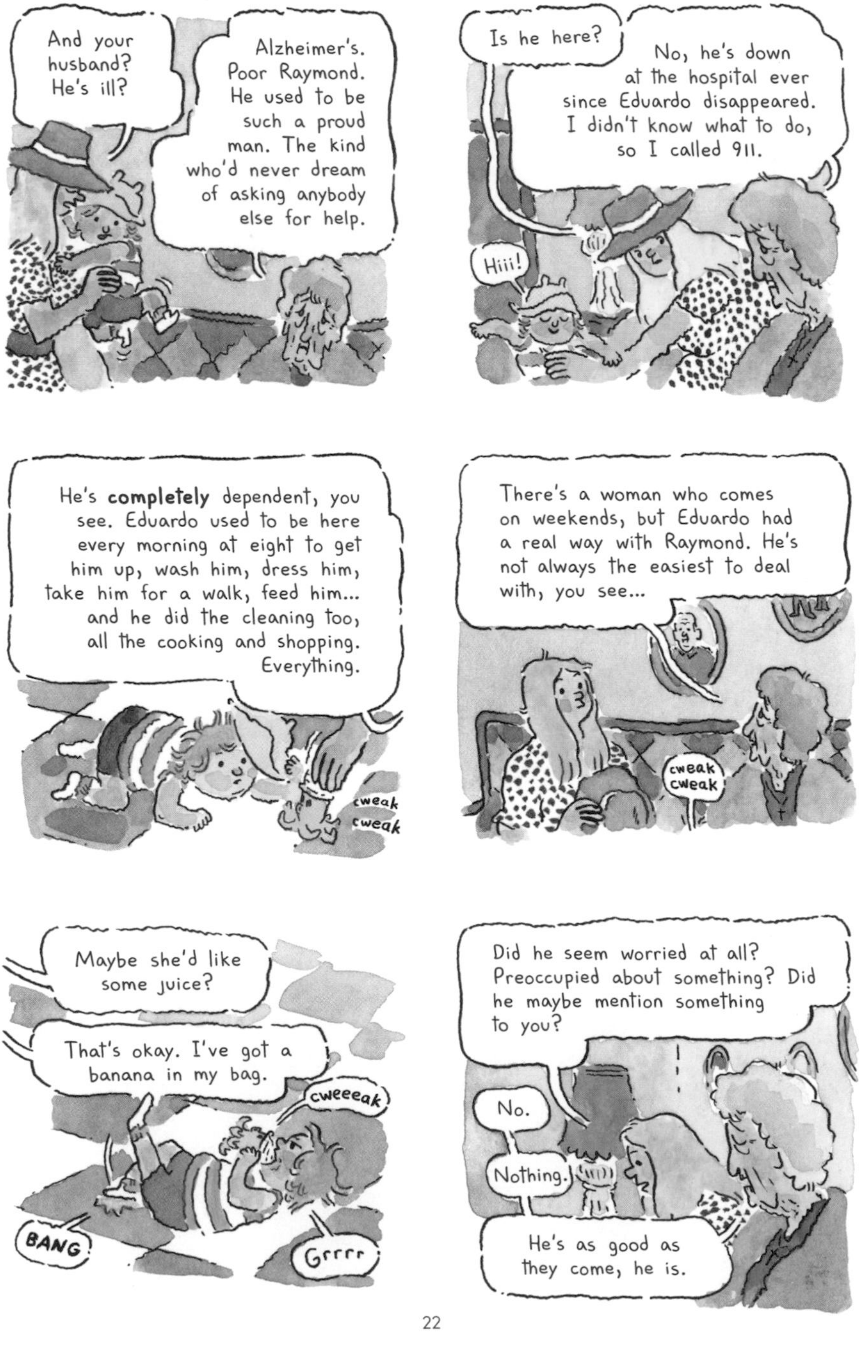
And your husband? He's ill?
Alzheimer's. Poor Raymond. He used to be such a proud man. The kind who'd never dream of asking anybody else for help.
Is he here?
No, he's down at the hospital ever since Eduardo disappeared. I didn't know what to do, so I called 911.
Hiii!
He's **completely** dependent, you see. Eduardo used to be here every morning at eight to get him up, wash him, dress him, take him for a walk, feed him... and he did the cleaning too, all the cooking and shopping. Everything.
cweak
cweak
There's a woman who comes on weekends, but Eduardo had a real way with Raymond. He's not always the easiest to deal with, you see...
cweak
cweak
Maybe she'd like some juice?
That's okay. I've got a banana in my bag.
cweeeak
BANG
Grrrr
Did he seem worried at all? Preoccupied about something? Did he maybe mention something to you?
No.
Nothing.
He's as good as they come, he is.

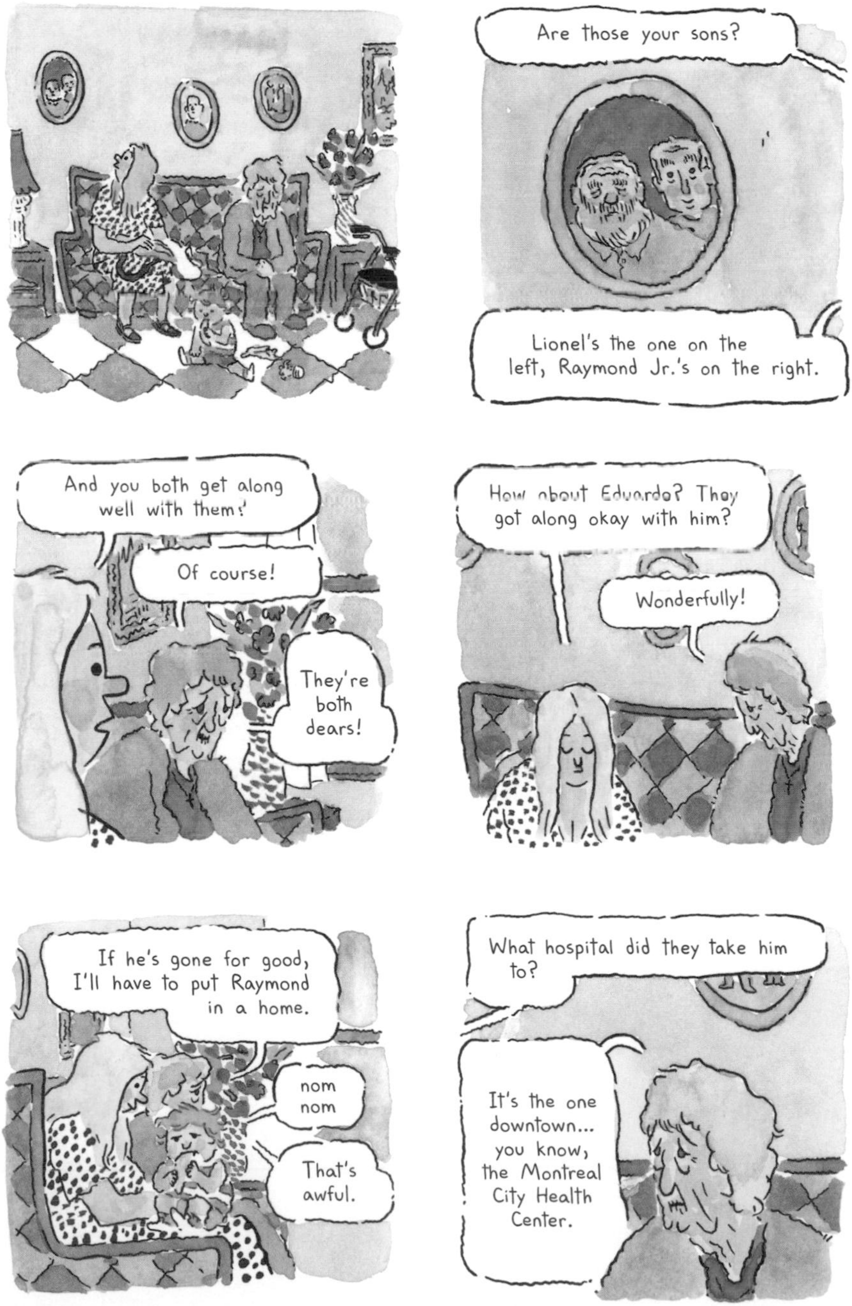

Are those your sons?
Lionel's the one on the left, Raymond Jr.'s on the right.
And you both get along well with them?
Of course!
They're both dears!
How about Eduardo? They got along okay with him?
Wonderfully!
If he's gone for good, I'll have to put Raymond in a home.
nom nom
That's awful.
What hospital did they take him to?
It's the one downtown... you know, the Montreal City Health Center.

Ha ha!
I can't believe it! She answered **all** of my questions!
It's honestly way easier than I thought.
And her husband is at Daddy's hospital! Can you believe it? Aren't we lucky?
Hehehehehe!
Gleh-gleh-gleh!
Hehehehe! Ah!
Obviously I can add the two sons to my list of suspects.
beeep
Let's just cross our fingers that they're as chatty as their mother.
Hey! Haha!
Lucie! No!
Sorry!

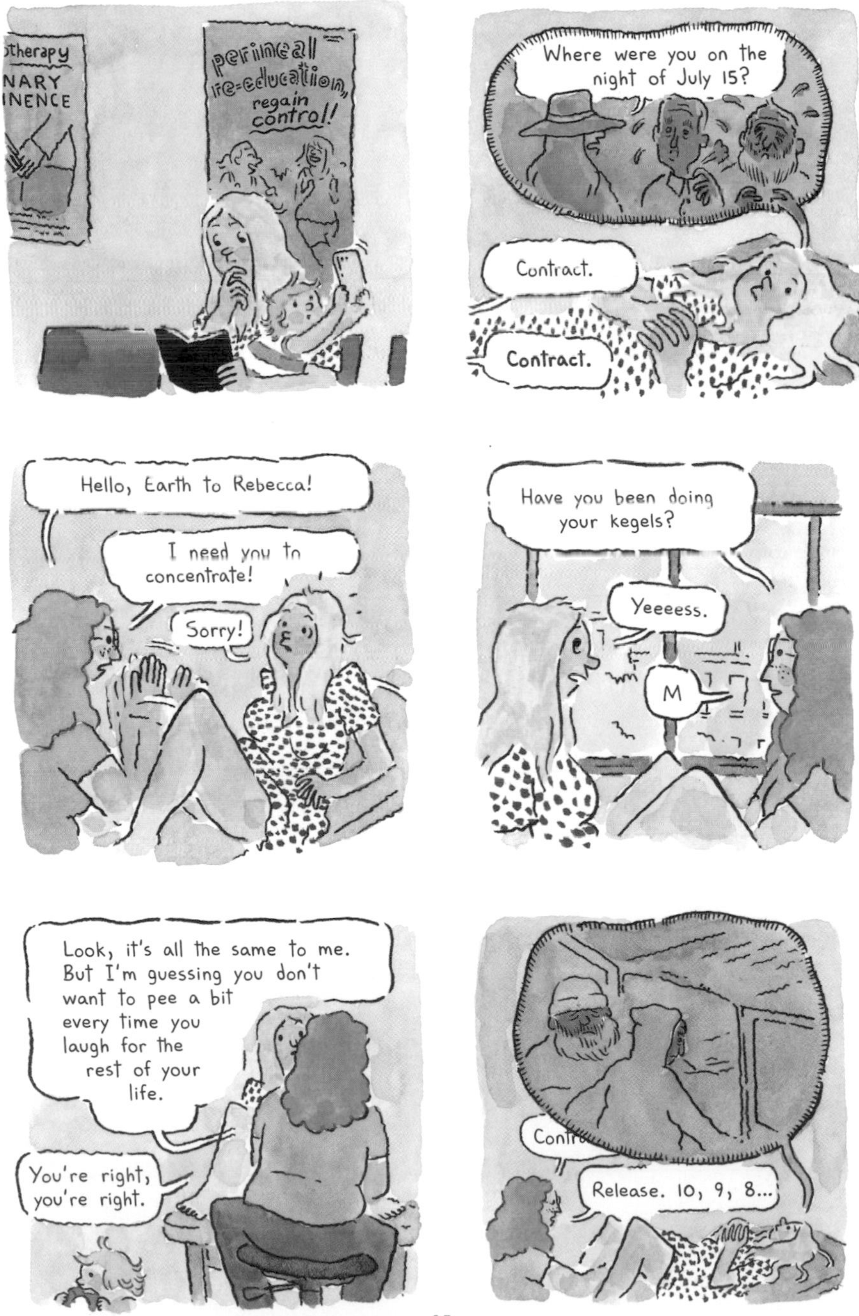
therapy
NARY
INENCE
perineal re-education, regain control!
Where were you on the night of July 15?
Contract.
Contract.
Hello, Earth to Rebecca!
I need you to concentrate!
Sorry!
Have you been doing your kegels?
Yeeeess.
M
Look, it's all the same to me. But I'm guessing you don't want to pee a bit every time you laugh for the rest of your life.
You're right, you're right.
Contr
Release. 10, 9, 8...

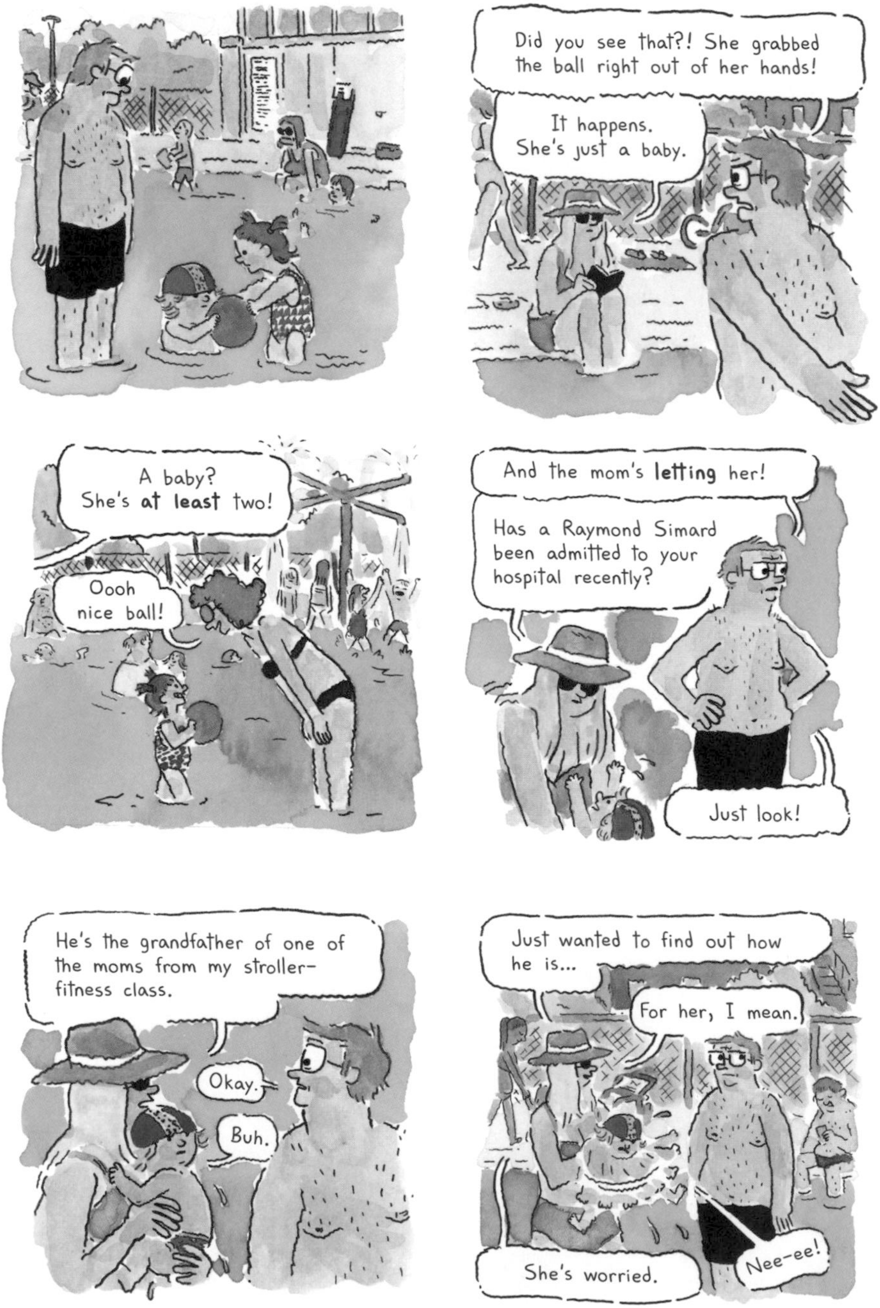
Did you see that?! She grabbed the ball right out of her hands!
It happens. She's just a baby.
A baby? She's **at least** two!
Oooh nice ball!
And the mom's **letting** her!
Has a Raymond Simard been admitted to your hospital recently?
Just look!
He's the grandfather of one of the moms from my stroller-fitness class.
Okay.
Buh.
Just wanted to find out how he is...
For her, I mean.
She's worried.
Nee-ee!

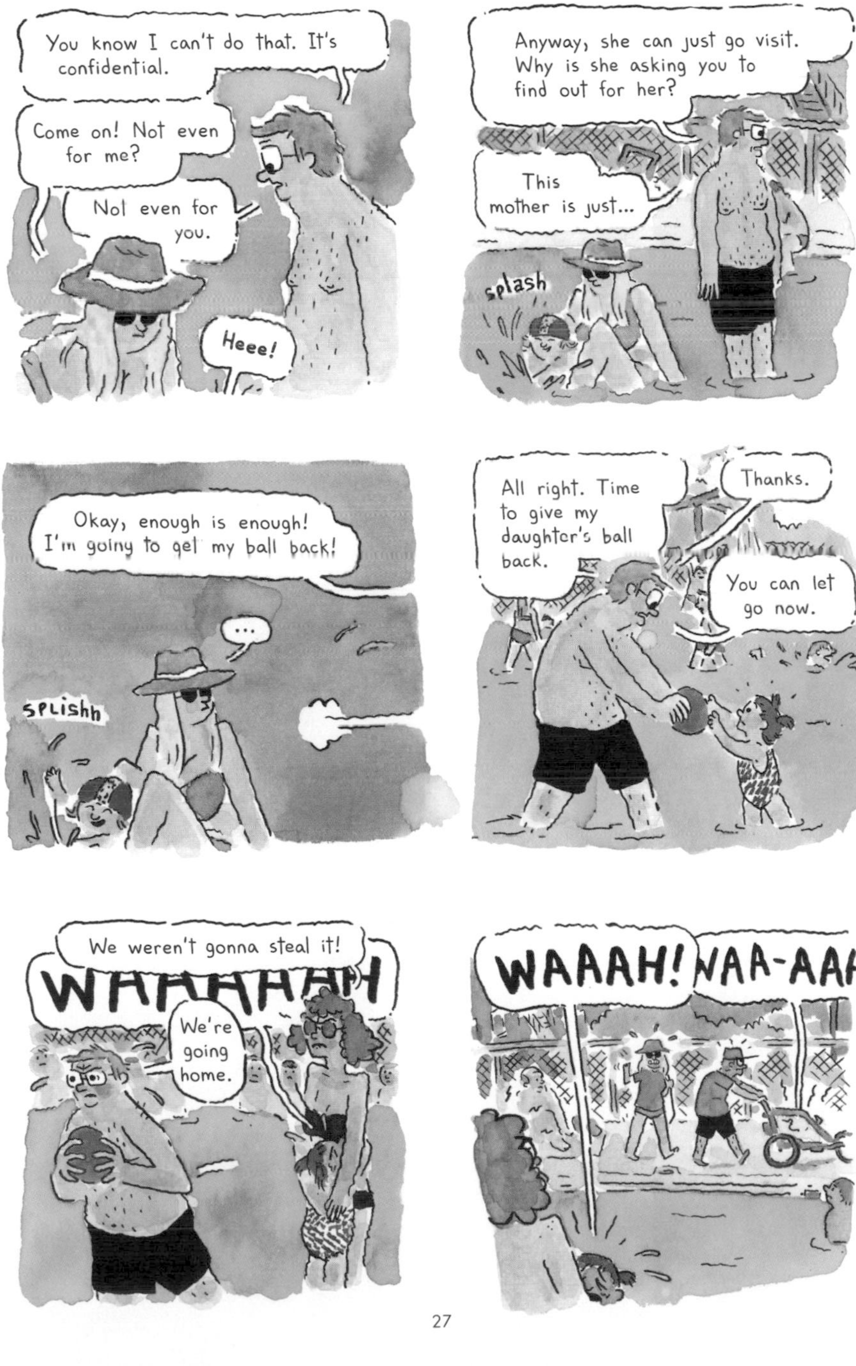
You know I can't do that. It's confidential.
Come on! Not even for me?
Not even for you.
Heee!
Anyway, she can just go visit. Why is she asking you to find out for her?
This mother is just...
splash
Okay, enough is enough! I'm going to get my ball back!
...
SPLISHH
All right. Time to give my daughter's ball back.
Thanks.
You can let go now.
We weren't gonna steal it!
WAAAAAH
We're going home.
WAAAH!
WAA-AA

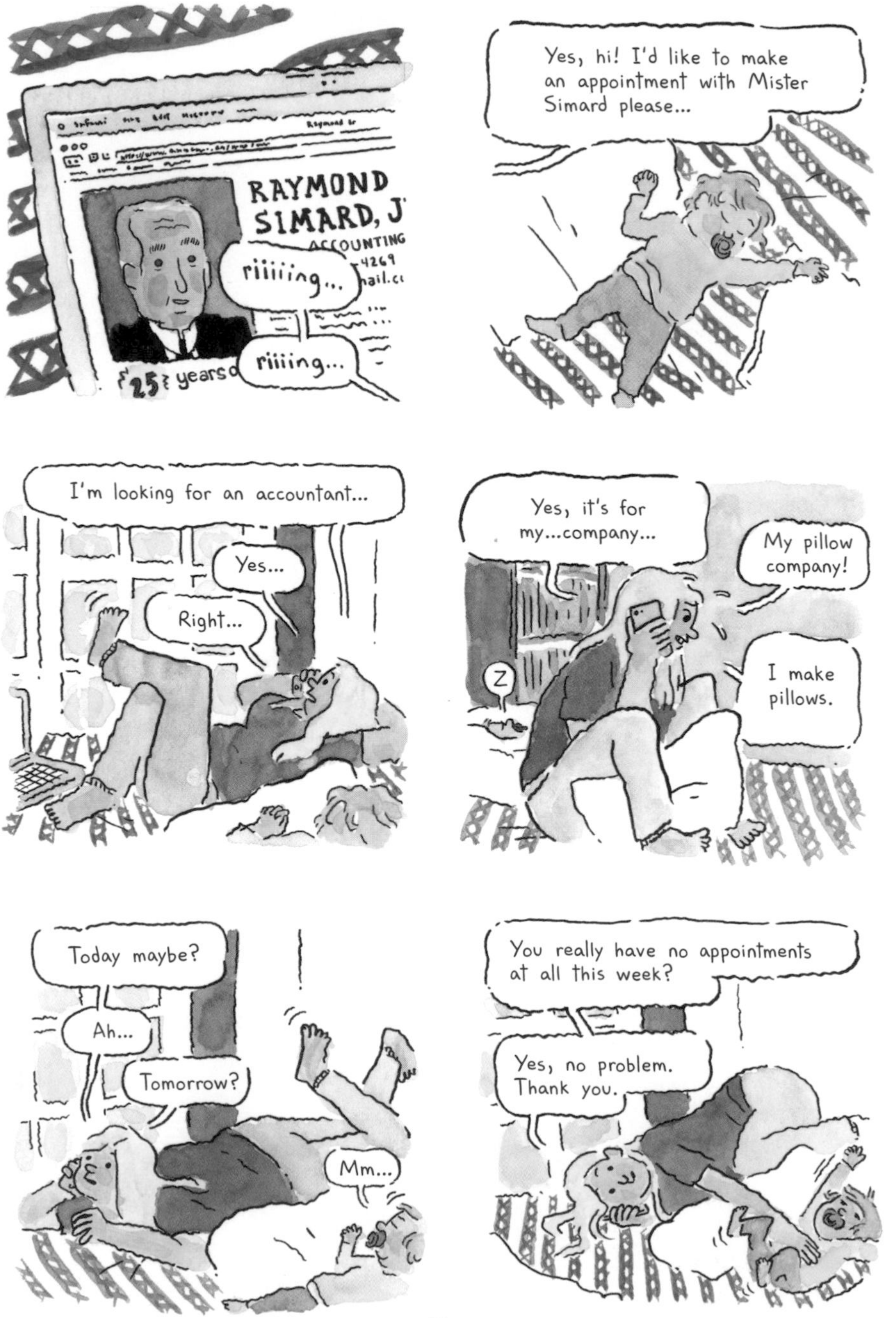
RAYMOND
SIMARD, J
ACCOUNTING
riiiiing...
riiiing...
Yes, hi! I'd like to make an appointment with Mister Simard please...
I'm looking for an accountant...
Right...
Yes...
Yes, it's for my...company...
My pillow company!
I make pillows.
Z
Today maybe?
Ah...
Tomorrow?
Mm...
You really have no appointments at all this week?
Yes, no problem. Thank you.

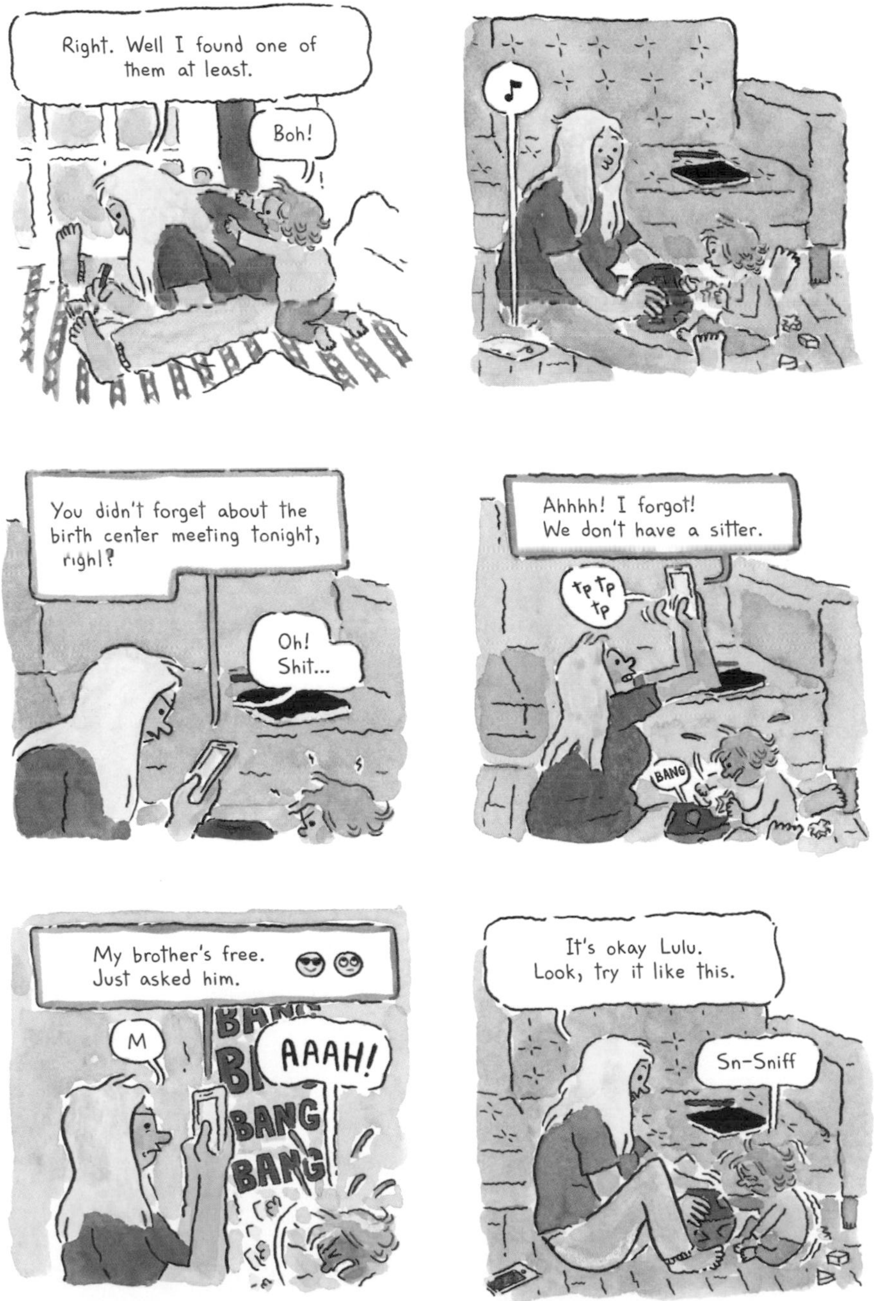

Right. Well I found one of them at least.
Boh!
You didn't forget about the birth center meeting tonight, right?
Oh! Shit...
Ahhhh! I forgot! We don't have a sitter.
tp tp tp
BANG
My brother's free. Just asked him.
M
AAAH!
BANG
BANG
It's okay Lulu. Look, try it like this.
Sn-Sniff

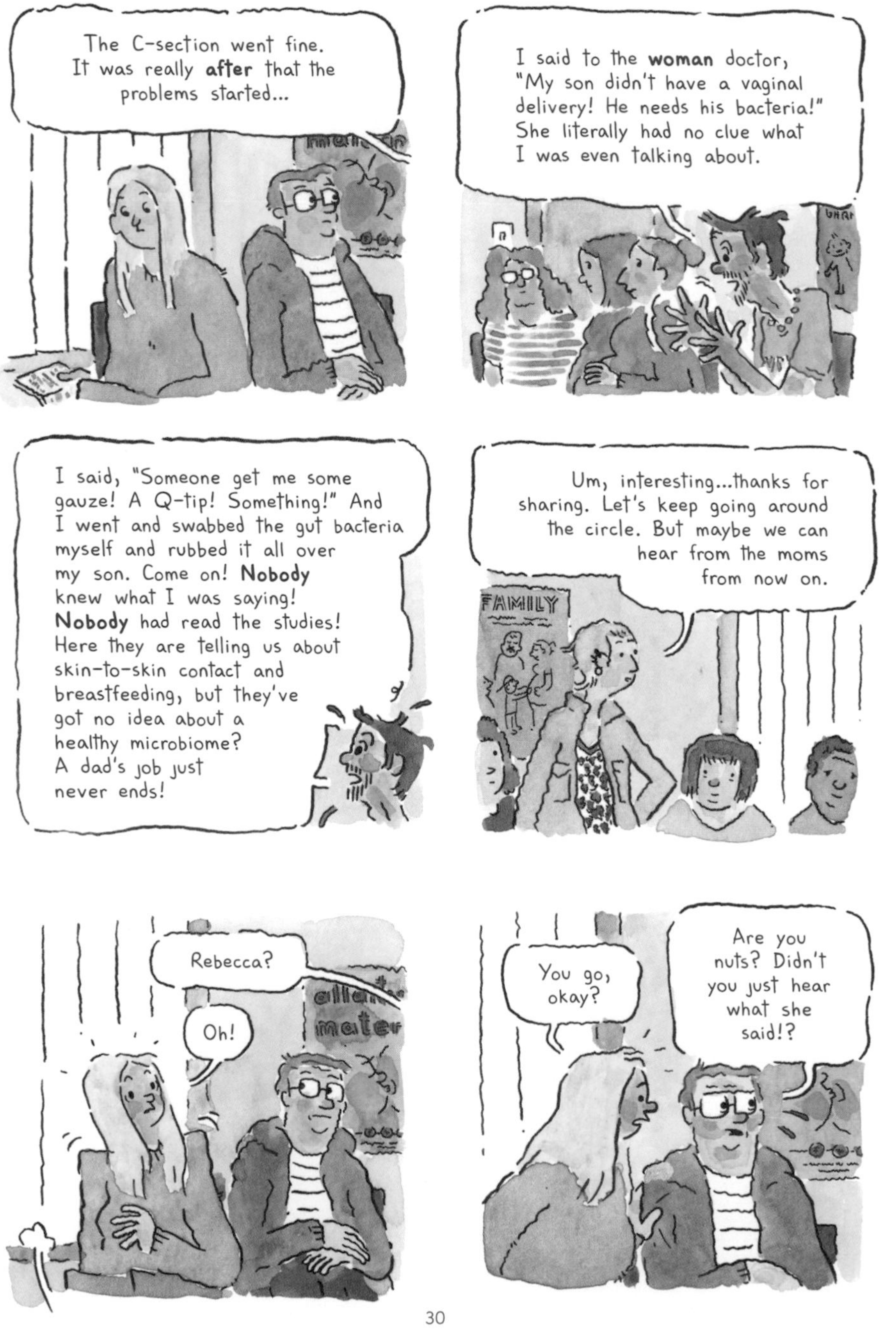

The C-section went fine. It was really **after** that the problems started...
I said to the **woman** doctor, "My son didn't have a vaginal delivery! He needs his bacteria!" She literally had no clue what I was even talking about.
I said, "Someone get me some gauze! A Q-tip! Something!" And I went and swabbed the gut bacteria myself and rubbed it all over my son. Come on! **Nobody** knew what I was saying! **Nobody** had read the studies! Here they are telling us about skin-to-skin contact and breastfeeding, but they've got no idea about a healthy microbiome? A dad's job just never ends!
FAMILY
Um, interesting...thanks for sharing. Let's keep going around the circle. But maybe we can hear from the moms from now on.
Rebecca?
Oh!
You go, okay?
Are you nuts? Didn't you just hear what she said!?

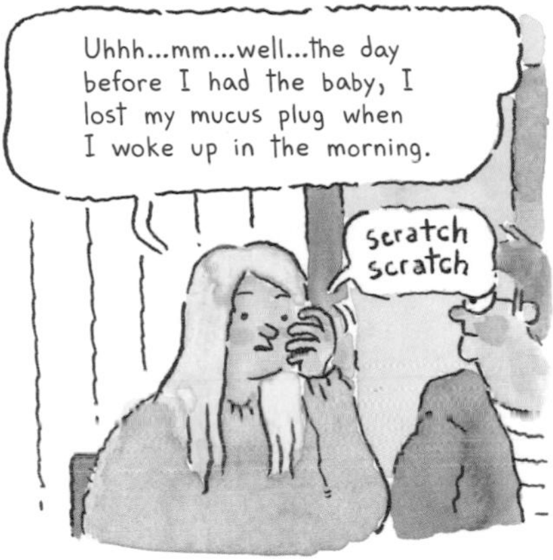
Uhhh...mm...well...the day before I had the baby, I lost my mucus plug when I woke up in the morning.
scratch scratch

I thought I'd peed the bed but I googled it and realized...

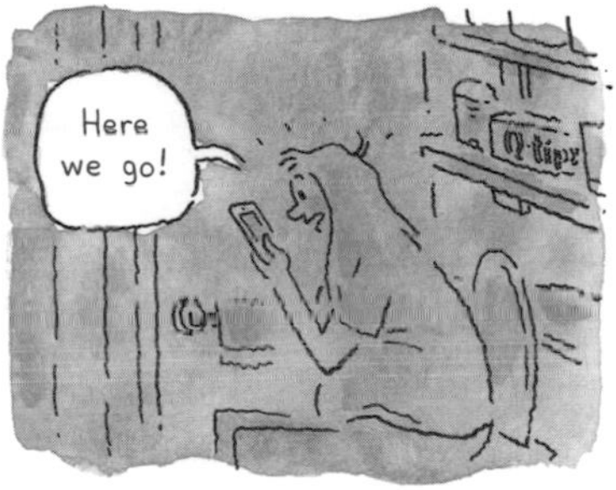
Here we go!

I didn't start having regular contractions until the evening.

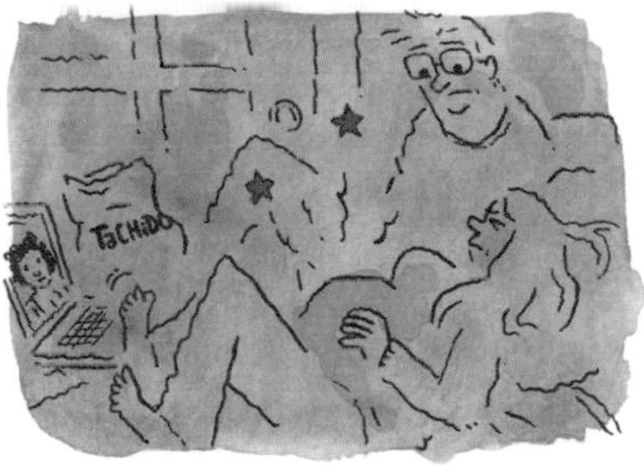

In between contractions I napped to conserve energy.

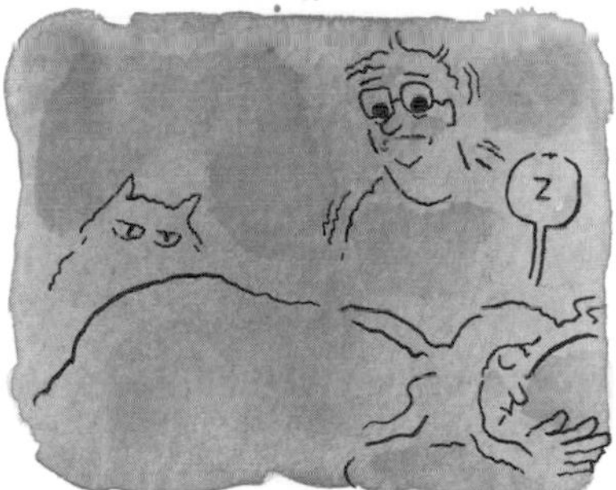
Z

We followed the five-one-one rule* before coming in at around three in the morning.

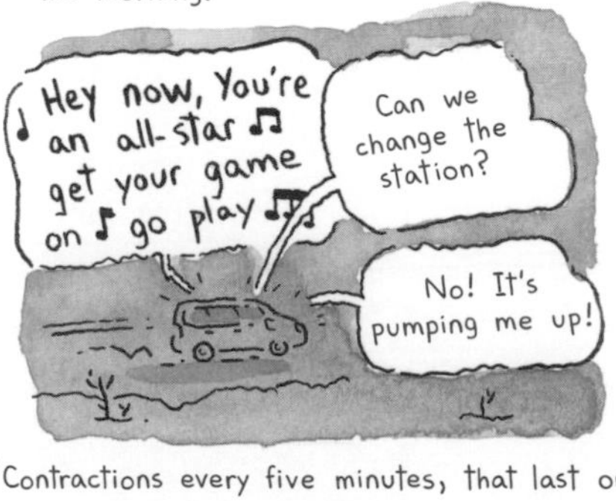
Hey now, You're an all-star get your game on go play
Can we change the station?
No! It's pumping me up!

I remember taking the elevator up to the second floor.

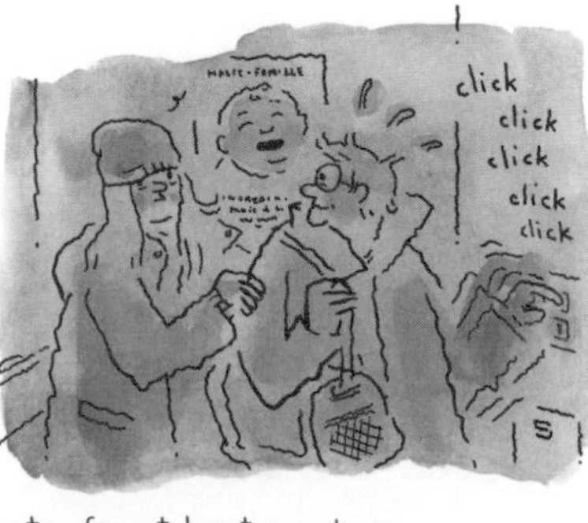
click click click click click

*Contractions every five minutes, that last one minute, for at least one hour.

My memory's a bit hazy after that...
I got undressed pretty fast.

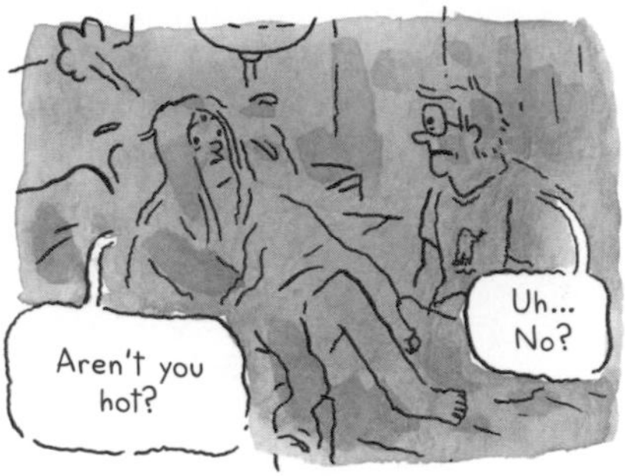
Uh... No?
Aren't you hot?

I spent a few hours
in the bath.

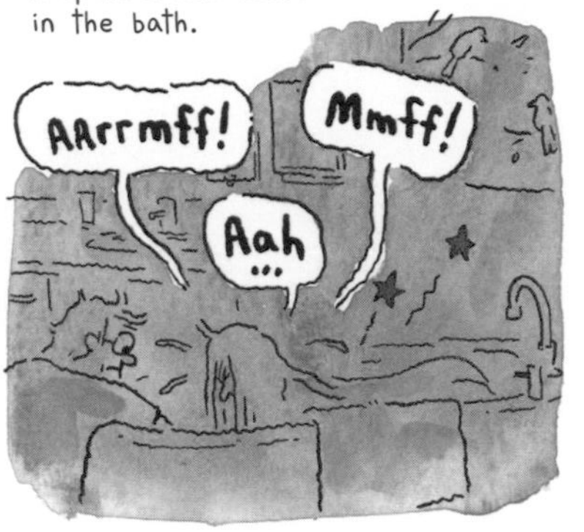
AArrmff!
Mmff!
Aah ...

I had the same mindset as when I run a marathon: giving up isn't an option; I have to make it to the finish line.

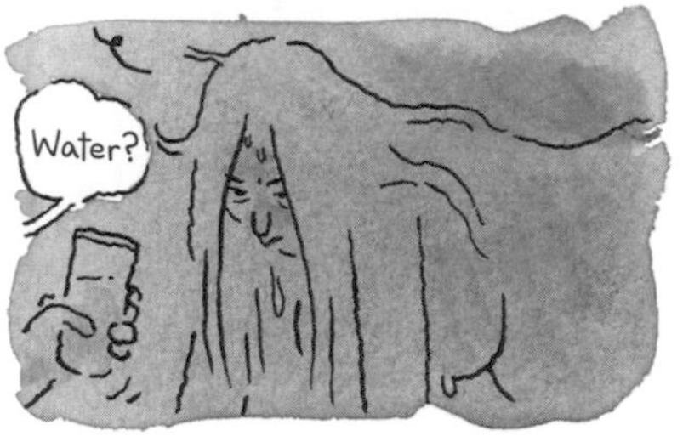
Water?

I remember sitting on an exercise ball and using some sort of swing.

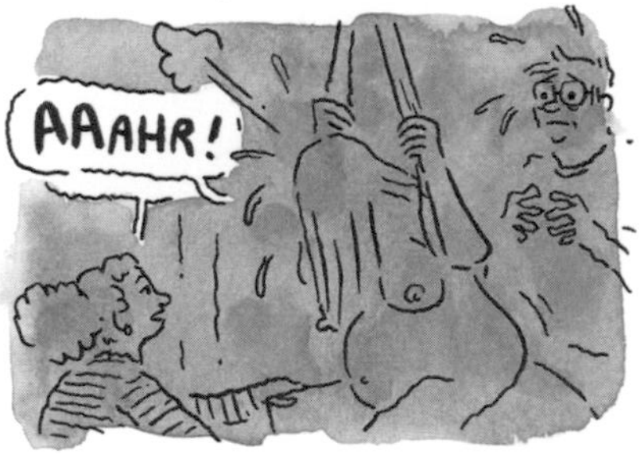
AAAHR!

The pushing part went fast.
Probably too fast.

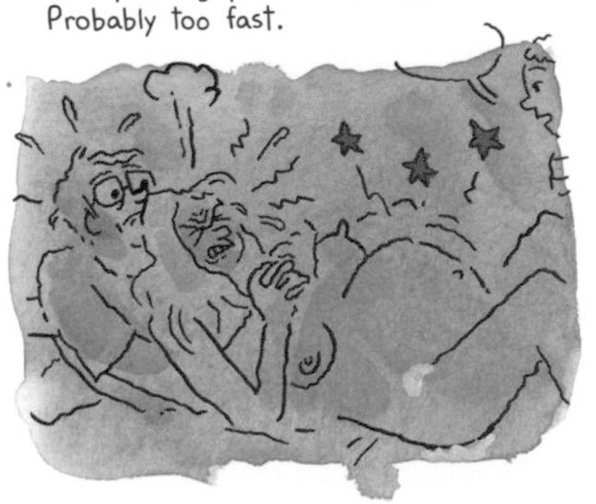

The midwife said to me:

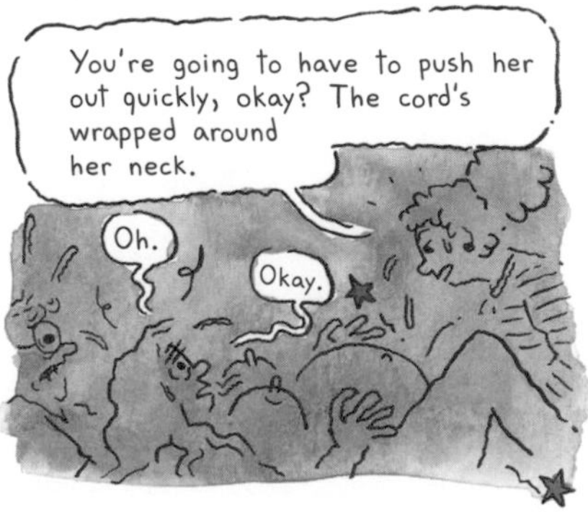
You're going to have to push her out quickly, okay? The cord's wrapped around her neck.
Oh.
Okay.

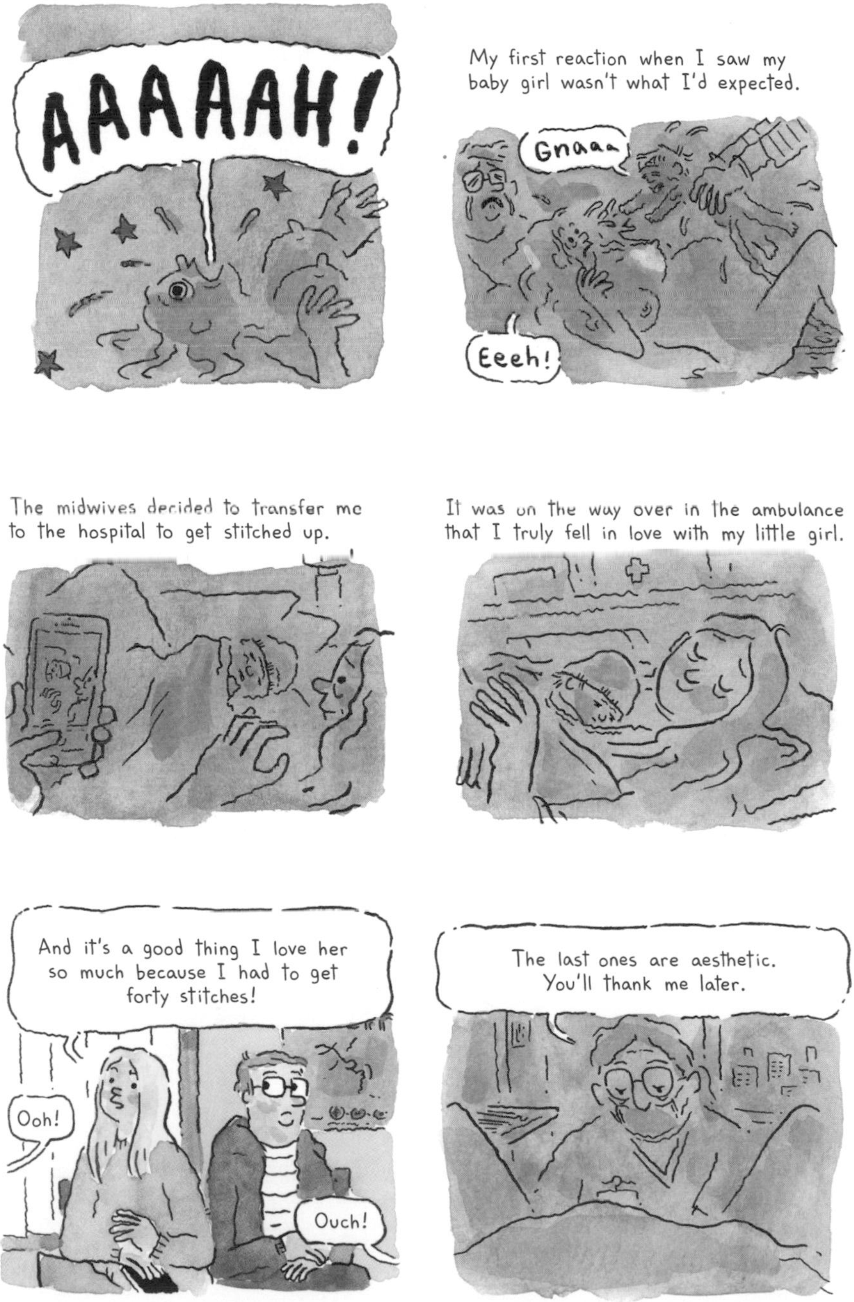
AAAAAH!
My first reaction when I saw my baby girl wasn't what I'd expected.
Gnaaa
Eeeh!
The midwives decided to transfer me to the hospital to get stitched up.
It was on the way over in the ambulance that I truly fell in love with my little girl.
And it's a good thing I love her so much because I had to get forty stitches!
Ooh!
Ouch!
The last ones are aesthetic. You'll thank me later.

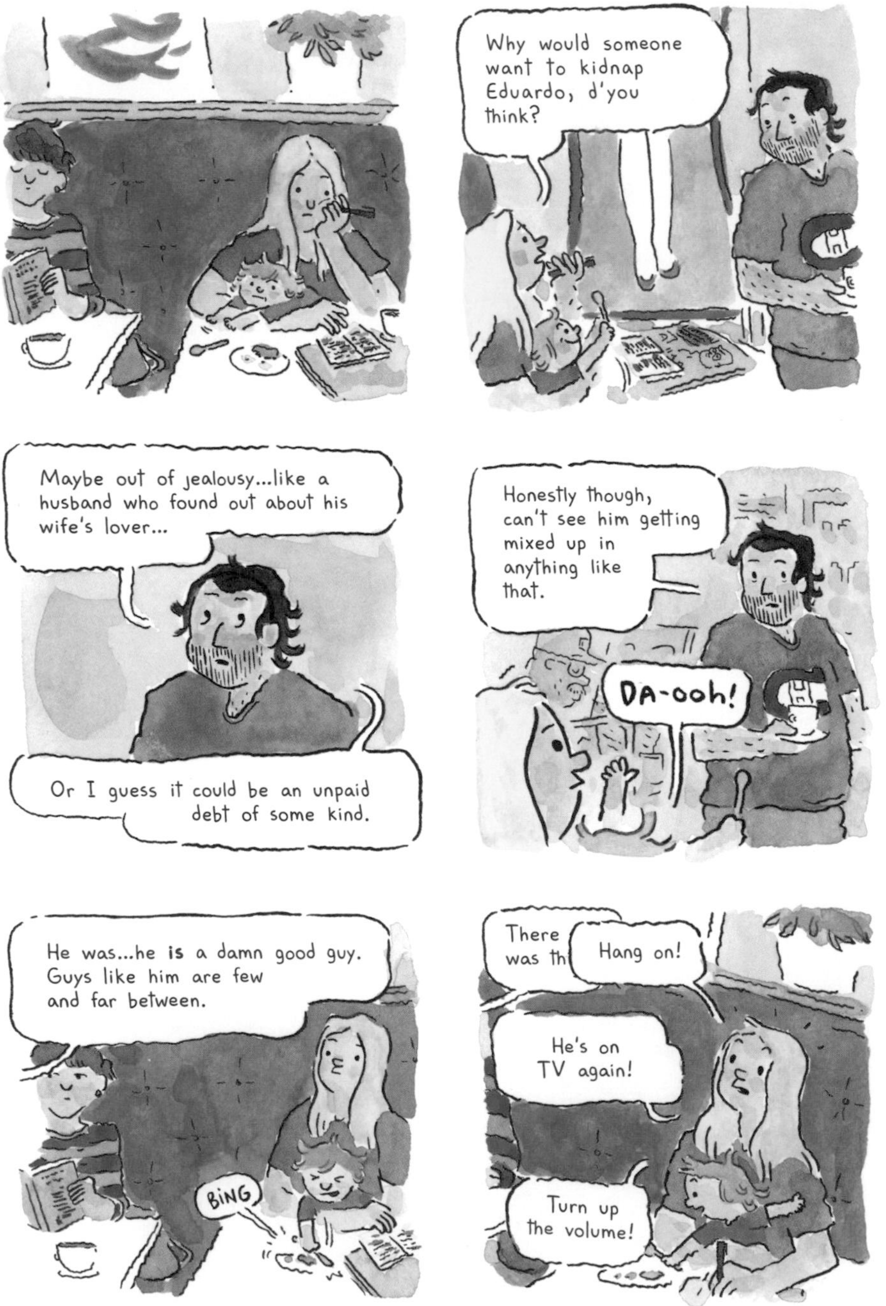

Why would someone want to kidnap Eduardo, d'you think?
Maybe out of jealousy...like a husband who found out about his wife's lover...
Or I guess it could be an unpaid debt of some kind.
Honestly though, can't see him getting mixed up in anything like that.
DA-ooh!
He was...he **is** a damn good guy. Guys like him are few and far between.
BING
There was th
Hang on!
He's on TV again!
Turn up the volume!

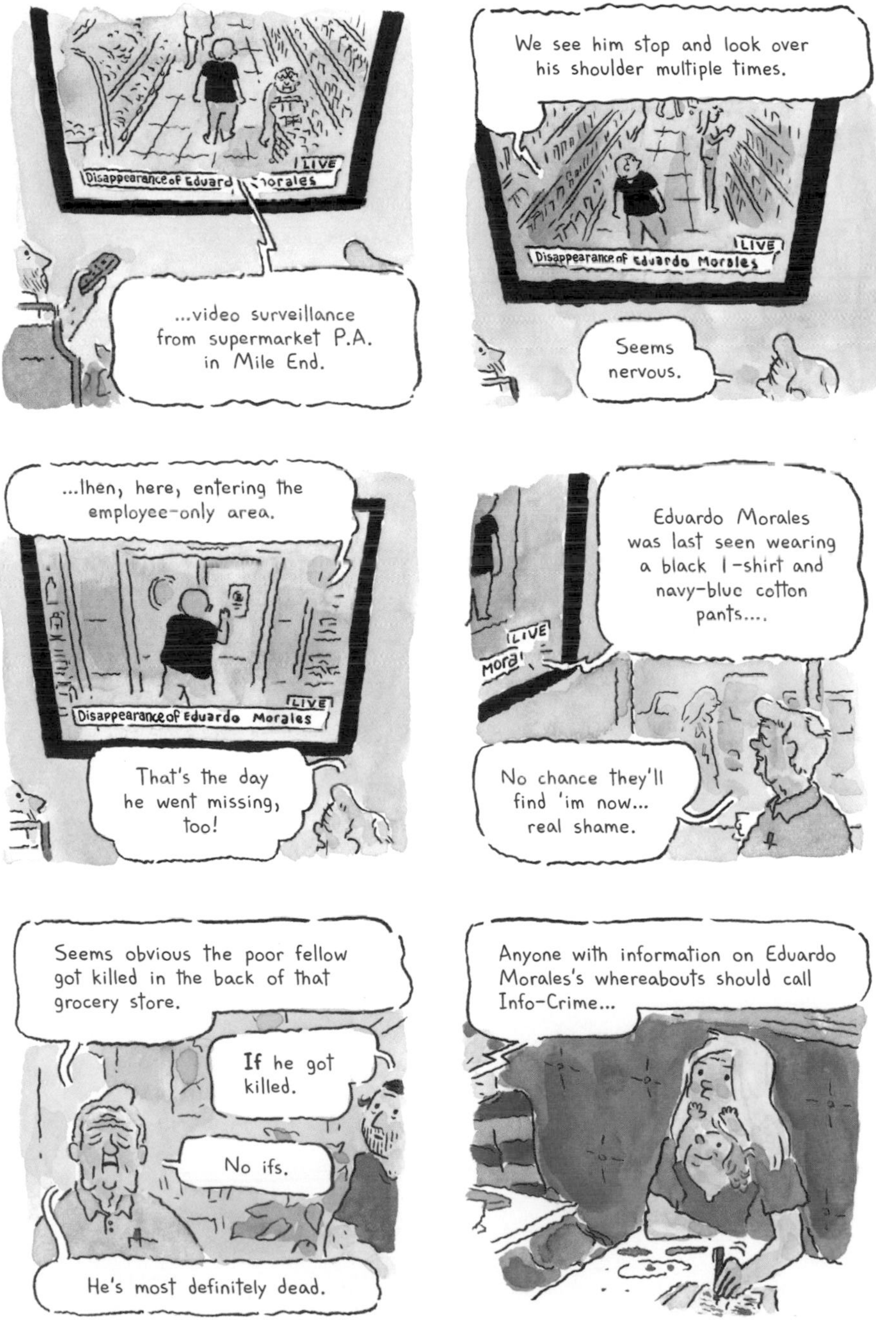
Disappearance of Eduard... orales
LIVE
...video surveillance from supermarket P.A. in Mile End.
We see him stop and look over his shoulder multiple times.
LIVE
Disappearance of Eduardo Morales
Seems nervous.
...then, here, entering the employee-only area.
LIVE
Disappearance of Eduardo Morales
That's the day he went missing, too!
Eduardo Morales was last seen wearing a black T-shirt and navy-blue cotton pants....
LIVE
Mora
No chance they'll find 'im now... real shame.
Seems obvious the poor fellow got killed in the back of that grocery store.
If he got killed.
No ifs.
He's most definitely dead.
Anyone with information on Eduardo Morales's whereabouts should call Info-Crime...

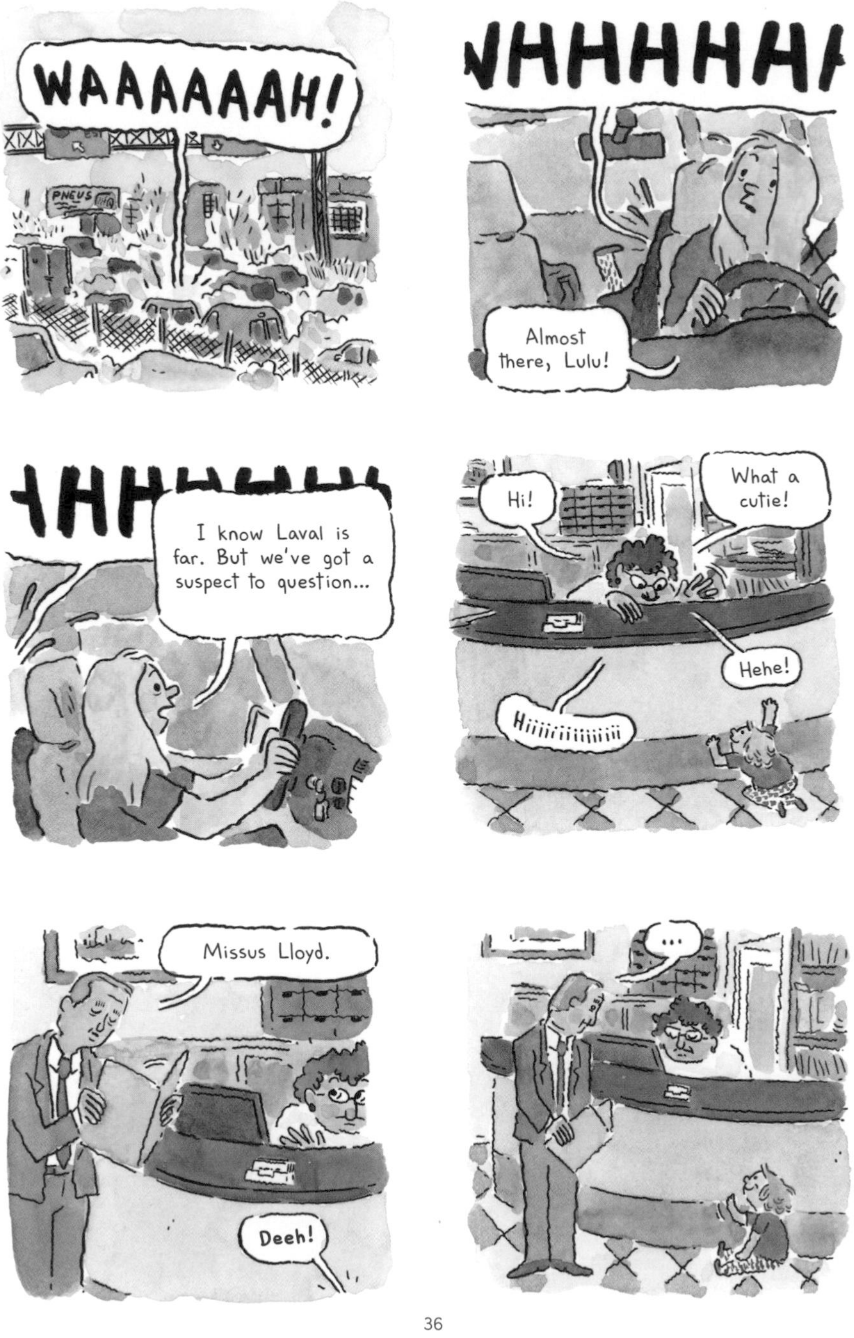
WAAAAAAH!
PNEUS
Almost there, Lulu!
I know Laval is far. But we've got a suspect to question...
Hi!
What a cutie!
Hehe!
Hiiiiiiiiiiiiiii
Missus Lloyd.
Deeh!
...

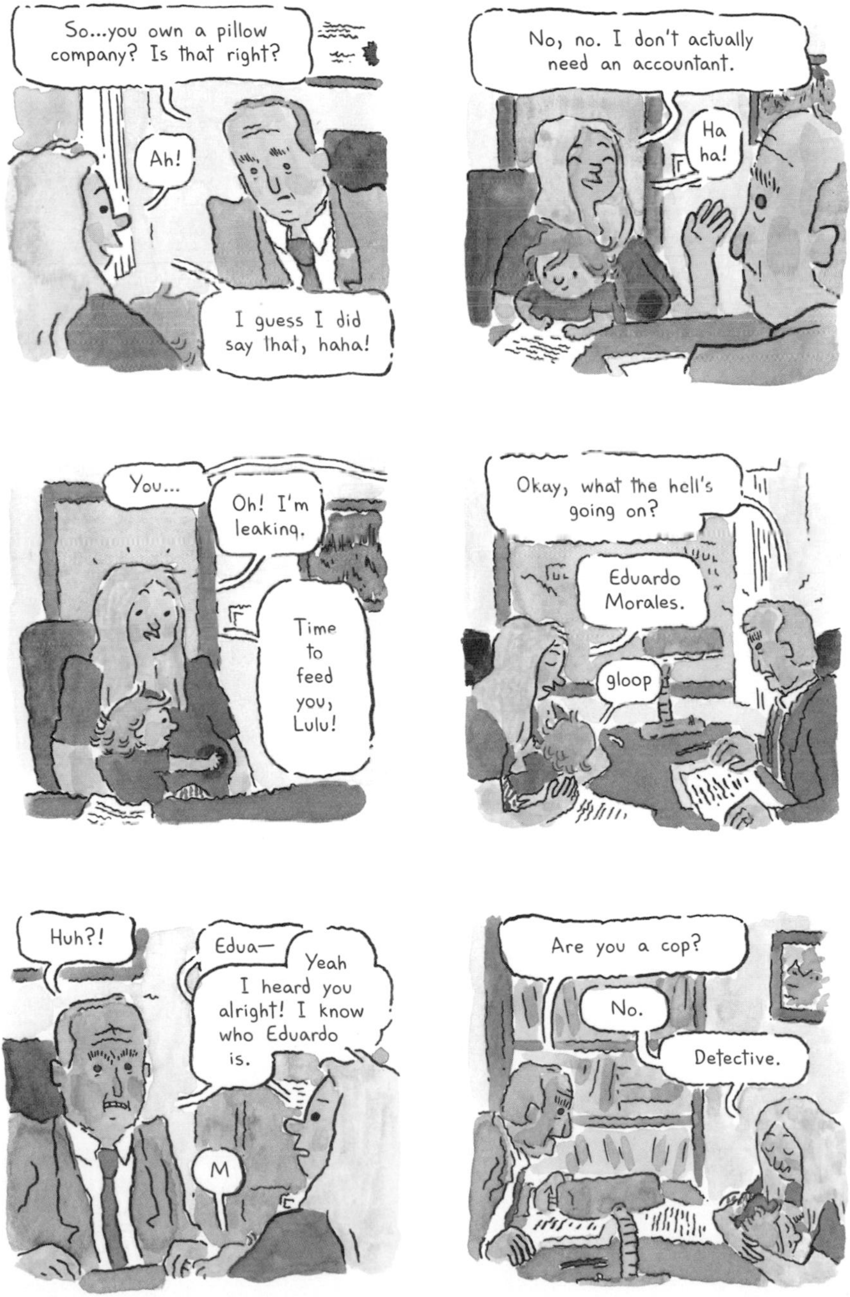
So...you own a pillow company? Is that right?
Ah!
I guess I did say that, haha!
No, no. I don't actually need an accountant.
Ha ha!
You...
Oh! I'm leaking.
Time to feed you, Lulu!
Okay, what the hell's going on?
Eduardo Morales.
gloop
Huh?!
Edua—
Yeah I heard you alright! I know who Eduardo is.
M
Are you a cop?
No.
Detective.

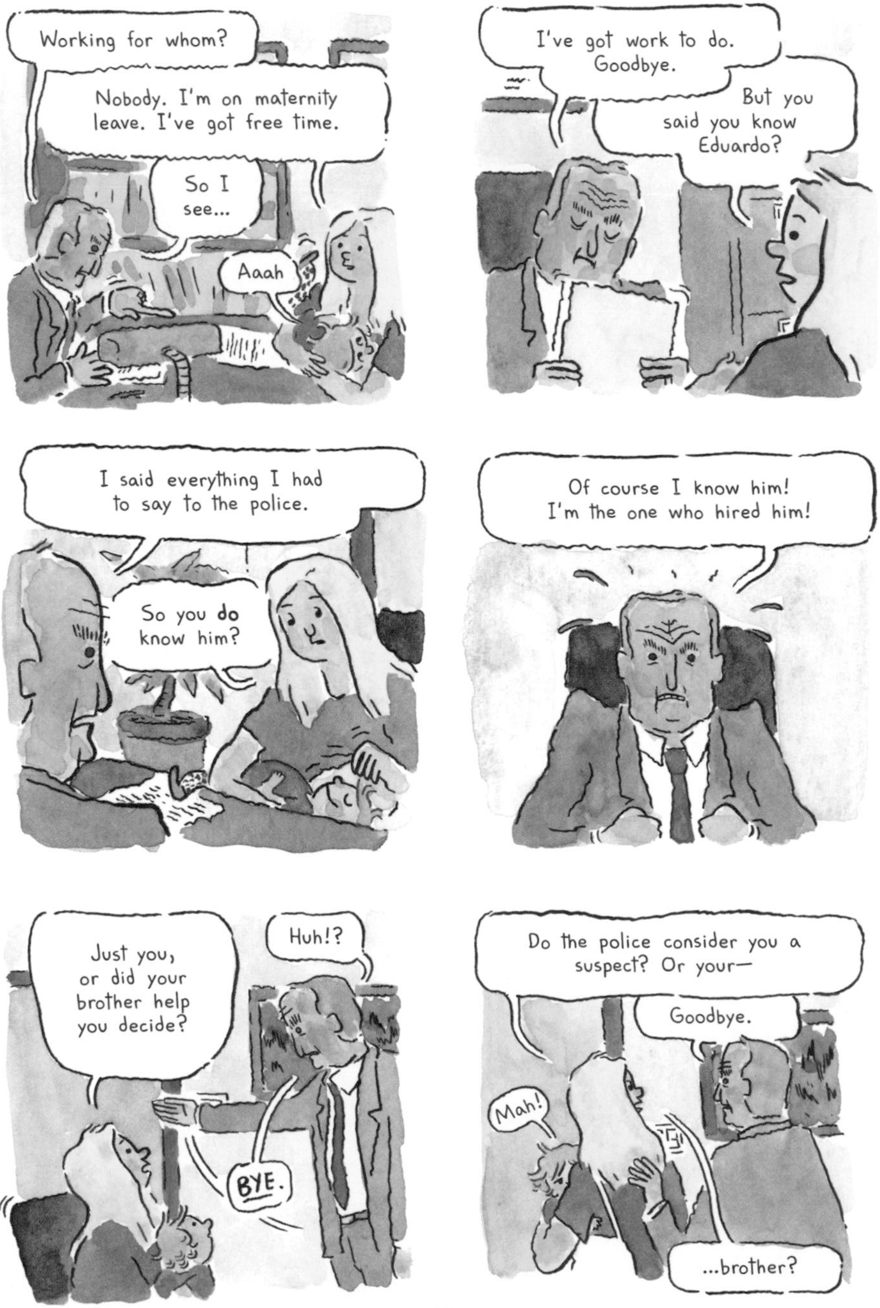
Working for whom?
Nobody. I'm on maternity leave. I've got free time.
So I see...
Aaah
I've got work to do. Goodbye.
But you said you know Eduardo?
I said everything I had to say to the police.
So you **do** know him?
Of course I know him! I'm the one who hired him!
Just you, or did your brother help you decide?
Huh!?
BYE.
Do the police consider you a suspect? Or your—
Goodbye.
Mah!
...brother?

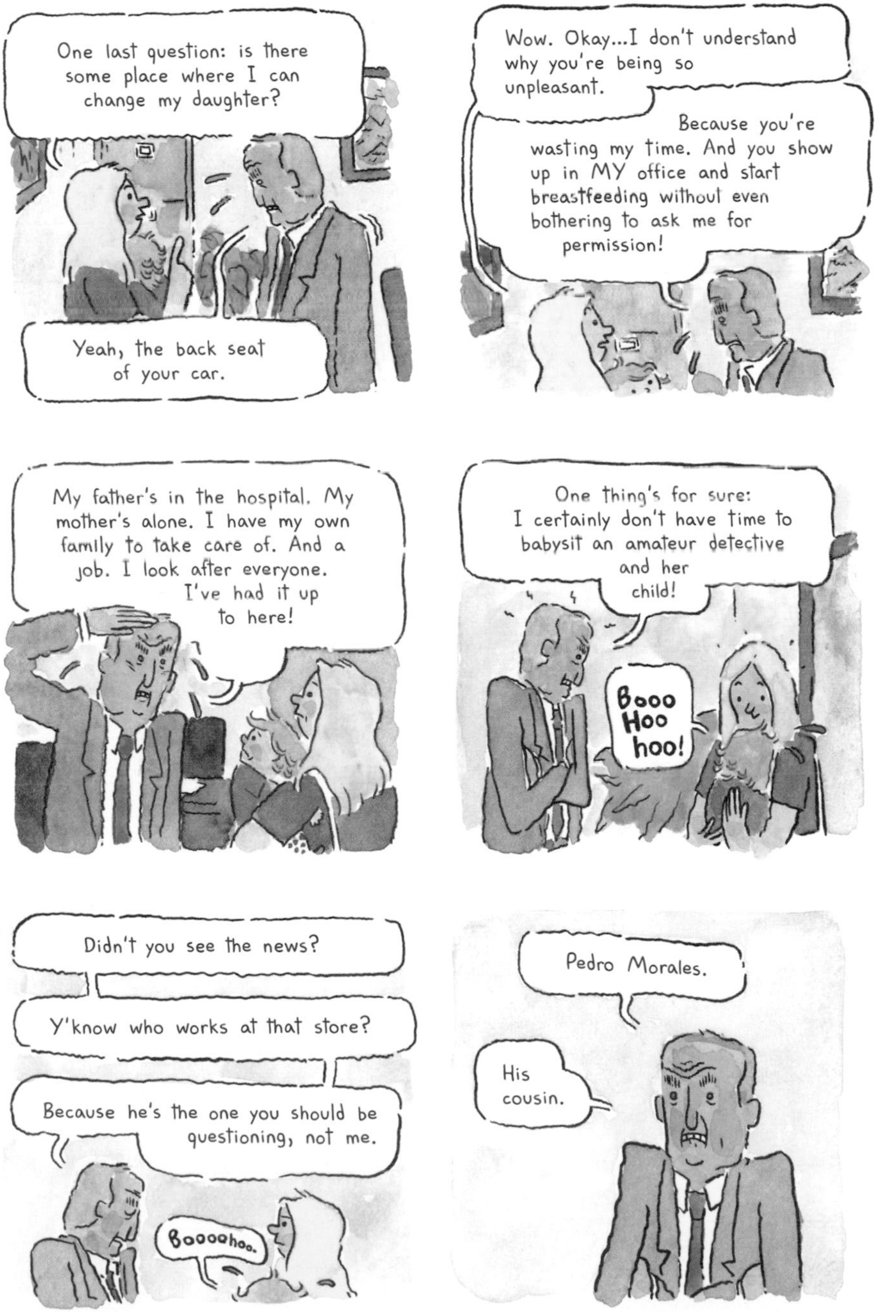
One last question: is there some place where I can change my daughter?
Yeah, the back seat of your car.
Wow. Okay...I don't understand why you're being so unpleasant.
Because you're wasting my time. And you show up in MY office and start breastfeeding without even bothering to ask me for permission!
My father's in the hospital. My mother's alone. I have my own family to take care of. And a job. I look after everyone. I've had it up to here!
One thing's for sure: I certainly don't have time to babysit an amateur detective and her child!
Booo Hoo hoo!
Didn't you see the news?
Y'know who works at that store?
Because he's the one you should be questioning, not me.
Booooho.
Pedro Morales.
His cousin.

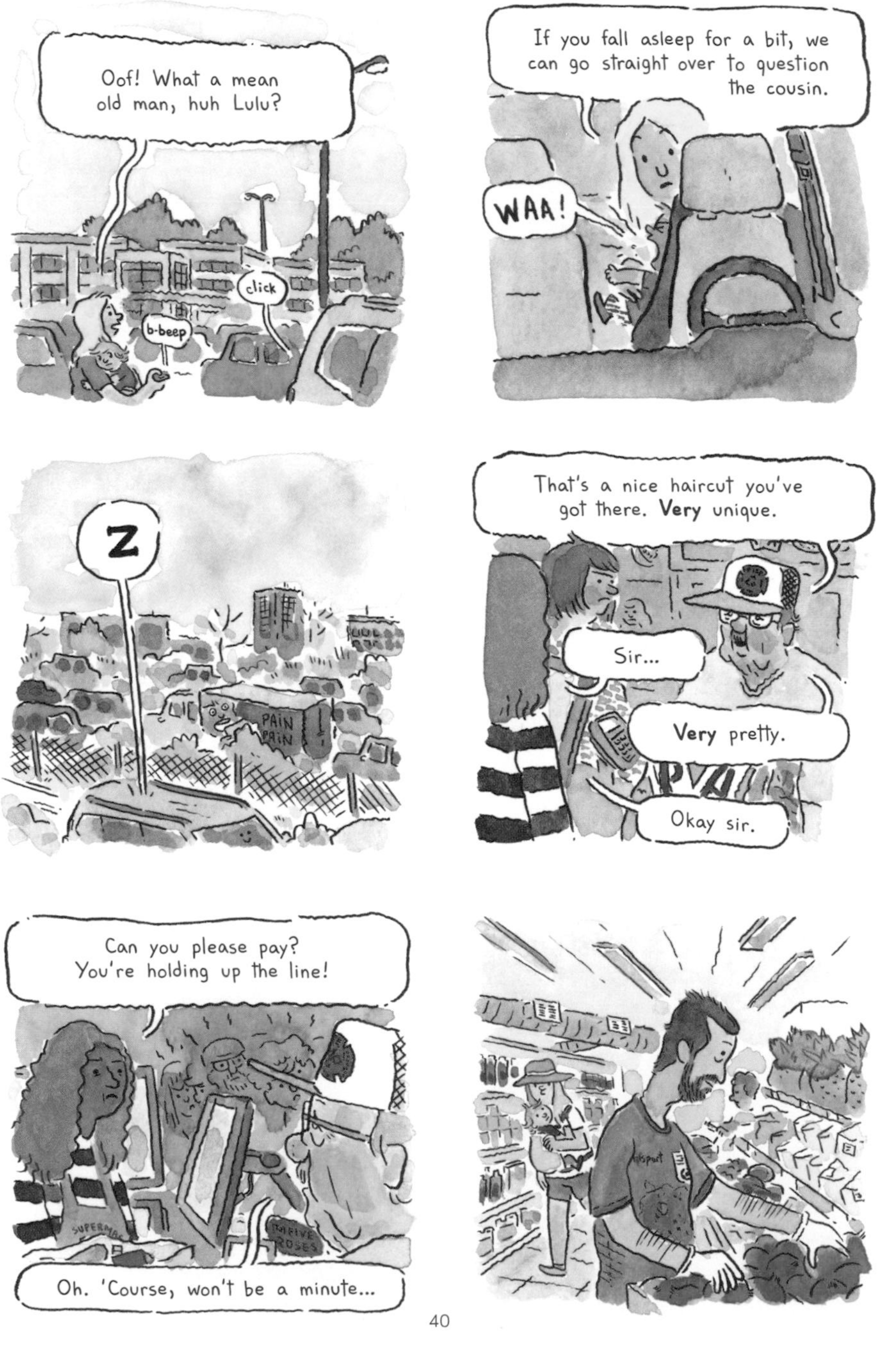

Oof! What a mean old man, huh Lulu?
click
b-beep
If you fall asleep for a bit, we can go straight over to question the cousin.
WAA!
Z
PAIN
PAIN
That's a nice haircut you've got there. **Very** unique.
Sir...
Very pretty.
Okay sir.
Can you please pay? You're holding up the line!
Oh. 'Course, won't be a minute...

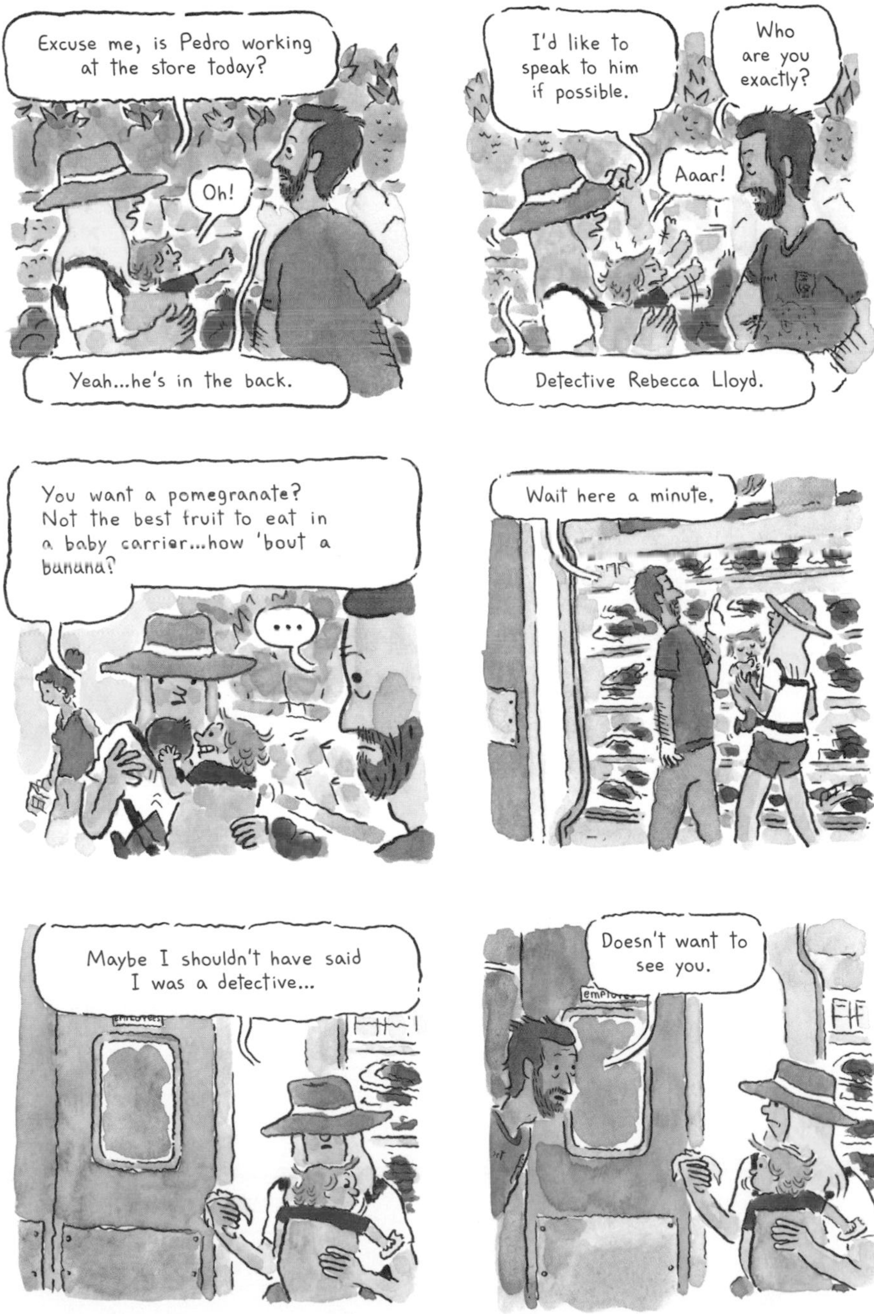
Excuse me, is Pedro working at the store today?
Oh!
Yeah...he's in the back.
I'd like to speak to him if possible.
Who are you exactly?
Aaar!
Detective Rebecca Lloyd.
You want a pomegranate? Not the best fruit to eat in a baby carrier...how 'bout a banana?
...
Wait here a minute.
Maybe I shouldn't have said I was a detective...
Doesn't want to see you.

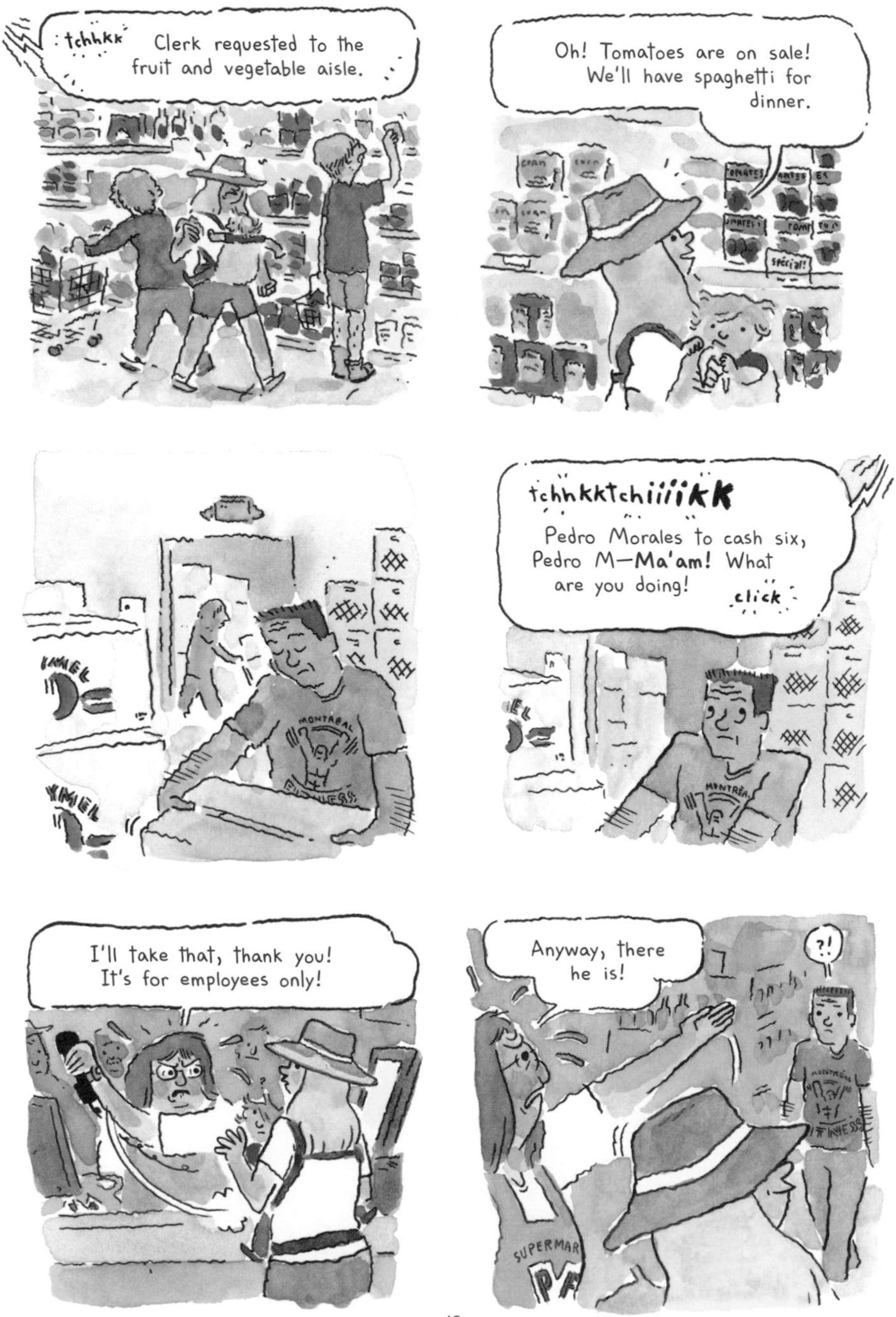
tchhkk Clerk requested to the fruit and vegetable aisle.
Oh! Tomatoes are on sale! We'll have spaghetti for dinner.
tchhkktchiiiikk
Pedro Morales to cash six, Pedro M—**Ma'am!** What are you doing!
click
I'll take that, thank you! It's for employees only!
Anyway, there he is!
?!

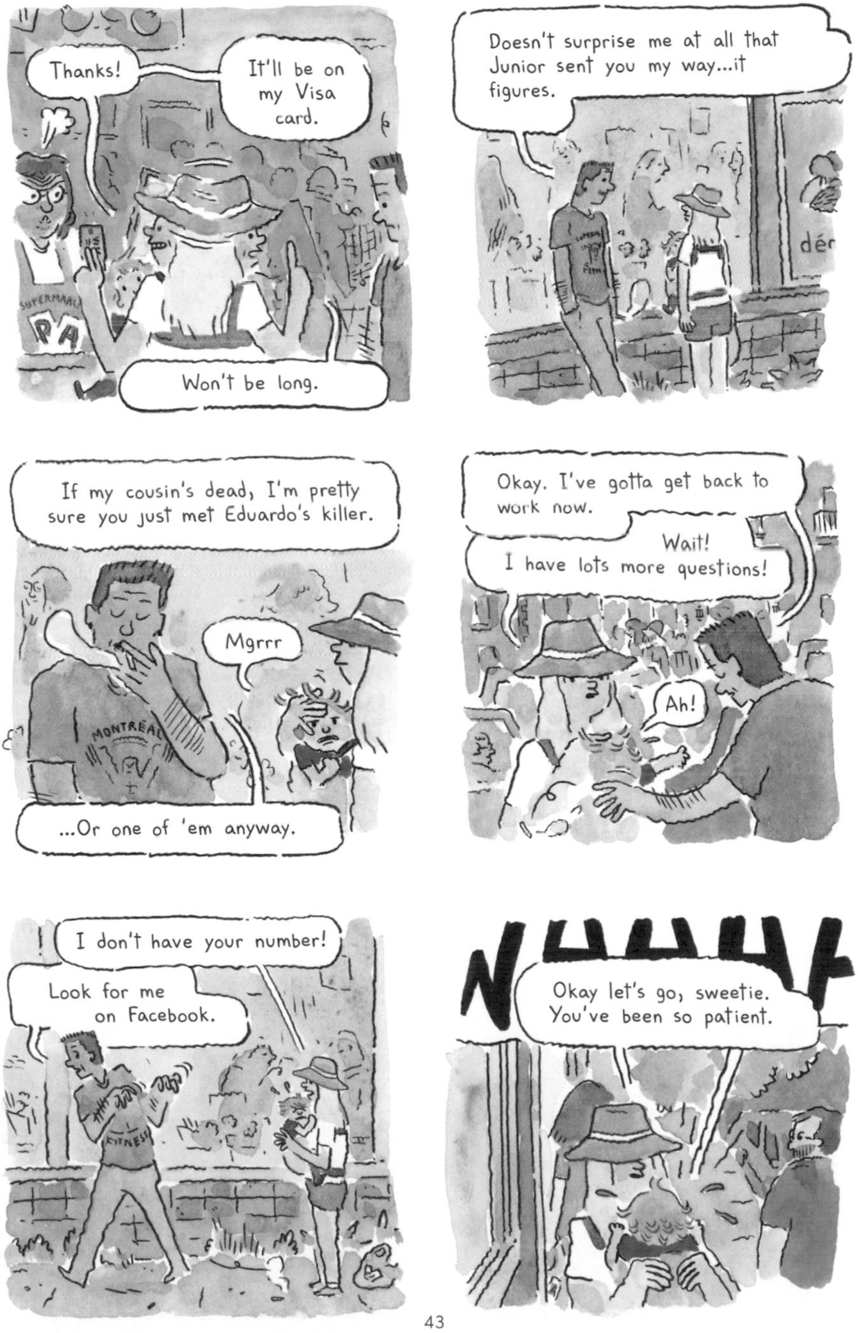
Thanks!
It'll be on my Visa card.
Won't be long.
Doesn't surprise me at all that Junior sent you my way...it figures.
If my cousin's dead, I'm pretty sure you just met Eduardo's killer.
Mgrrr
MONTREAL
...Or one of 'em anyway.
Okay. I've gotta get back to work now.
Wait! I have lots more questions!
Ah!
I don't have your number!
Look for me on Facebook.
Okay let's go, sweetie. You've been so patient.

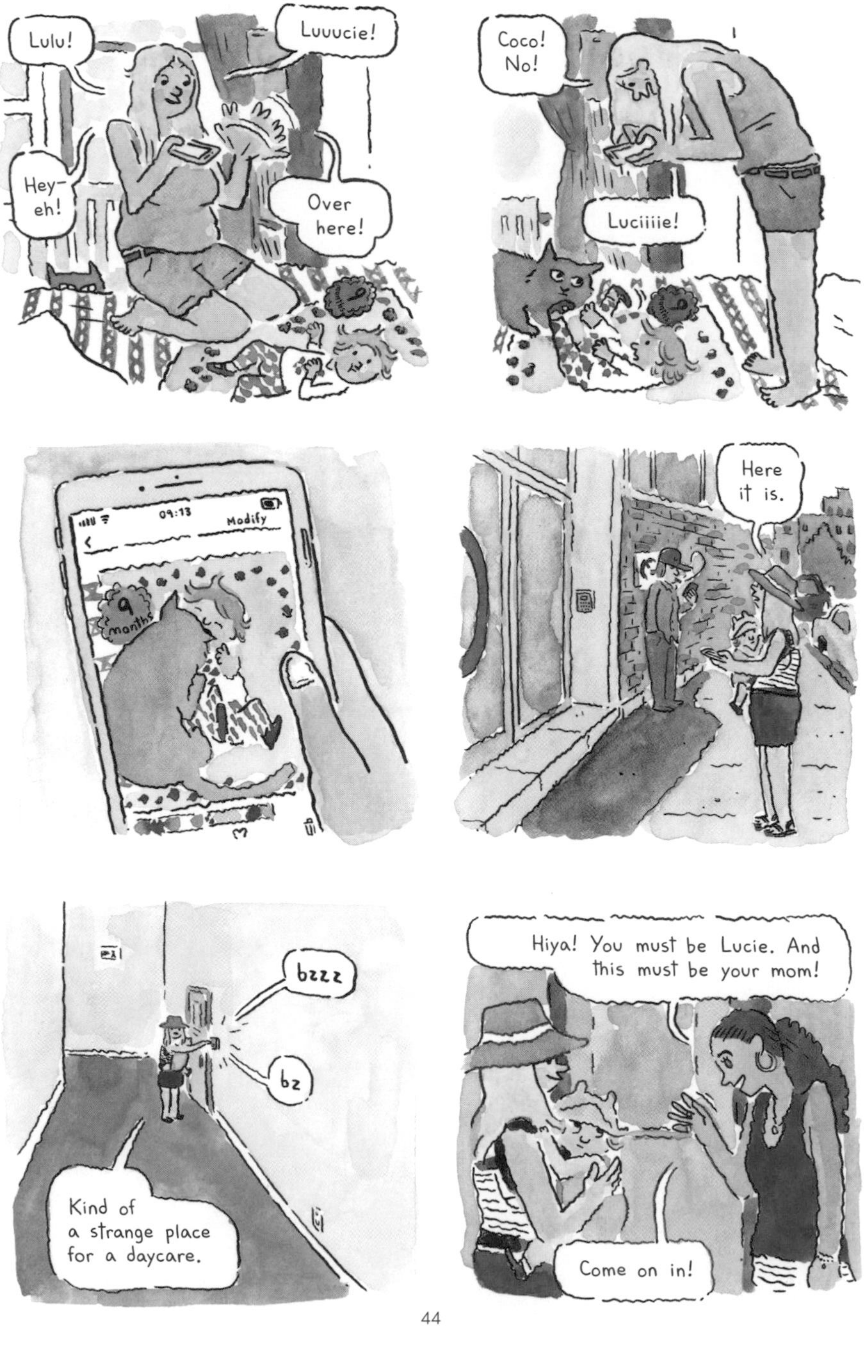
Lulu!
Luuucie!
Hey-eh!
Over here!
Coco! No!
Luciiiie!
09:13
Modify
9 months
Here it is.
bzzz
bz
Kind of a strange place for a daycare.
Hiya! You must be Lucie. And this must be your mom!
Come on in!

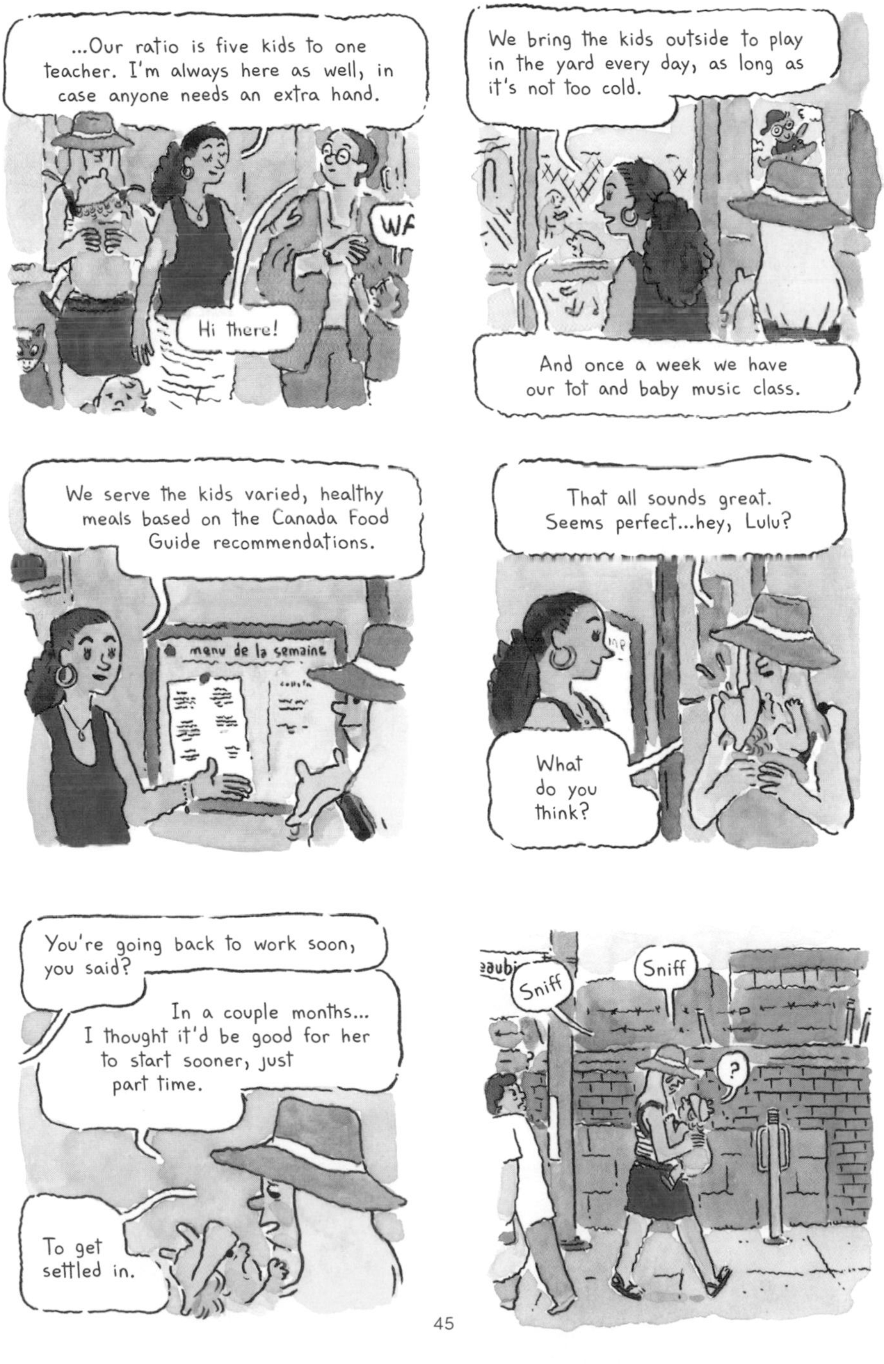
...Our ratio is five kids to one teacher. I'm always here as well, in case anyone needs an extra hand.
Hi there!
We bring the kids outside to play in the yard every day, as long as it's not too cold.
And once a week we have our tot and baby music class.
We serve the kids varied, healthy meals based on the Canada Food Guide recommendations.
menu de la semaine
That all sounds great. Seems perfect...hey, Lulu?
What do you think?
You're going back to work soon, you said?
In a couple months... I thought it'd be good for her to start sooner, just part time.
To get settled in.
Sniff
Sniff
?

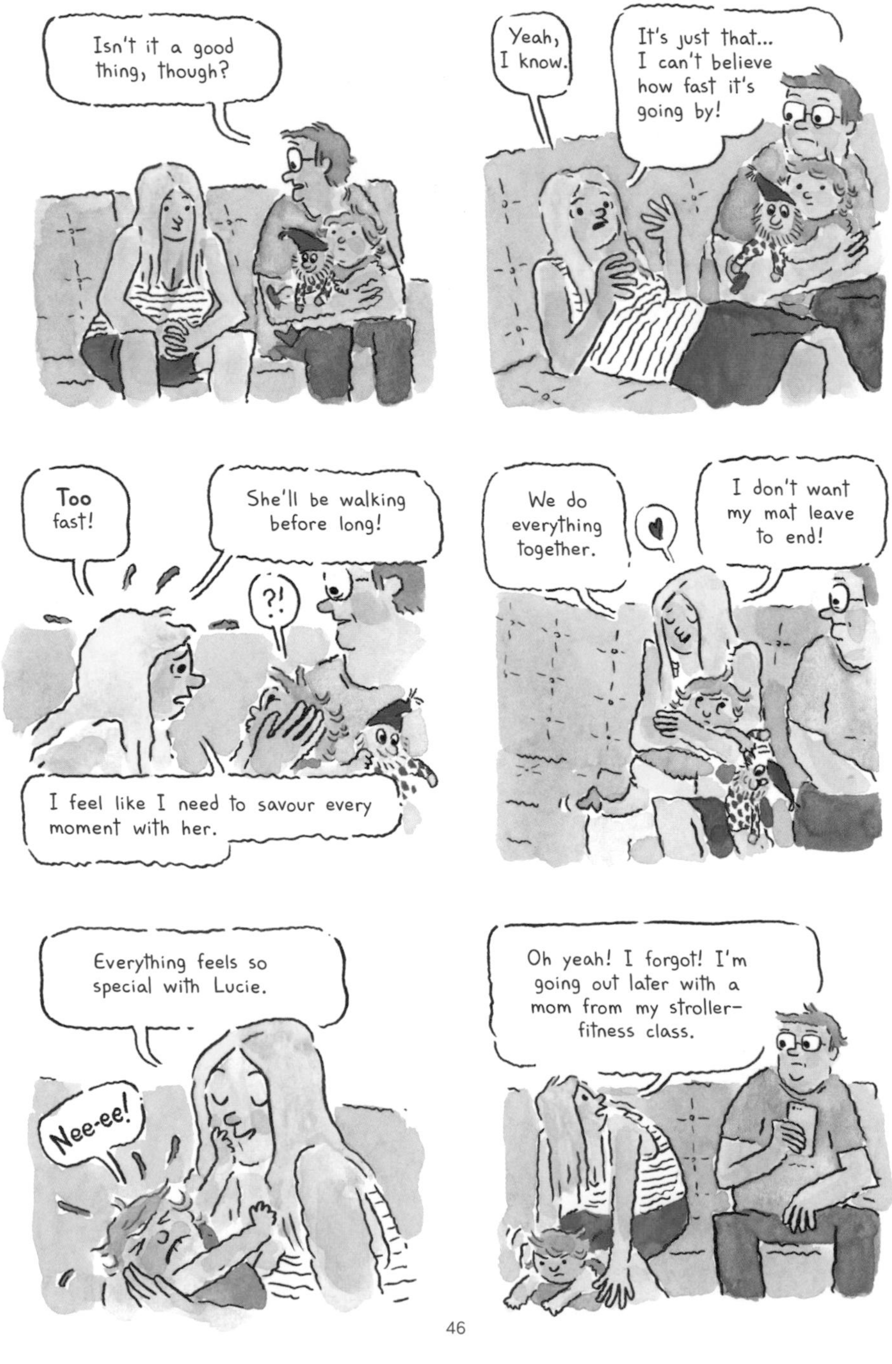
Isn't it a good thing, though?
Yeah, I know.
It's just that... I can't believe how fast it's going by!
Too fast!
She'll be walking before long!
?!
I feel like I need to savour every moment with her.
We do everything together.
I don't want my mat leave to end!
Everything feels so special with Lucie.
Nee-ee!
Oh yeah! I forgot! I'm going out later with a mom from my stroller-fitness class.

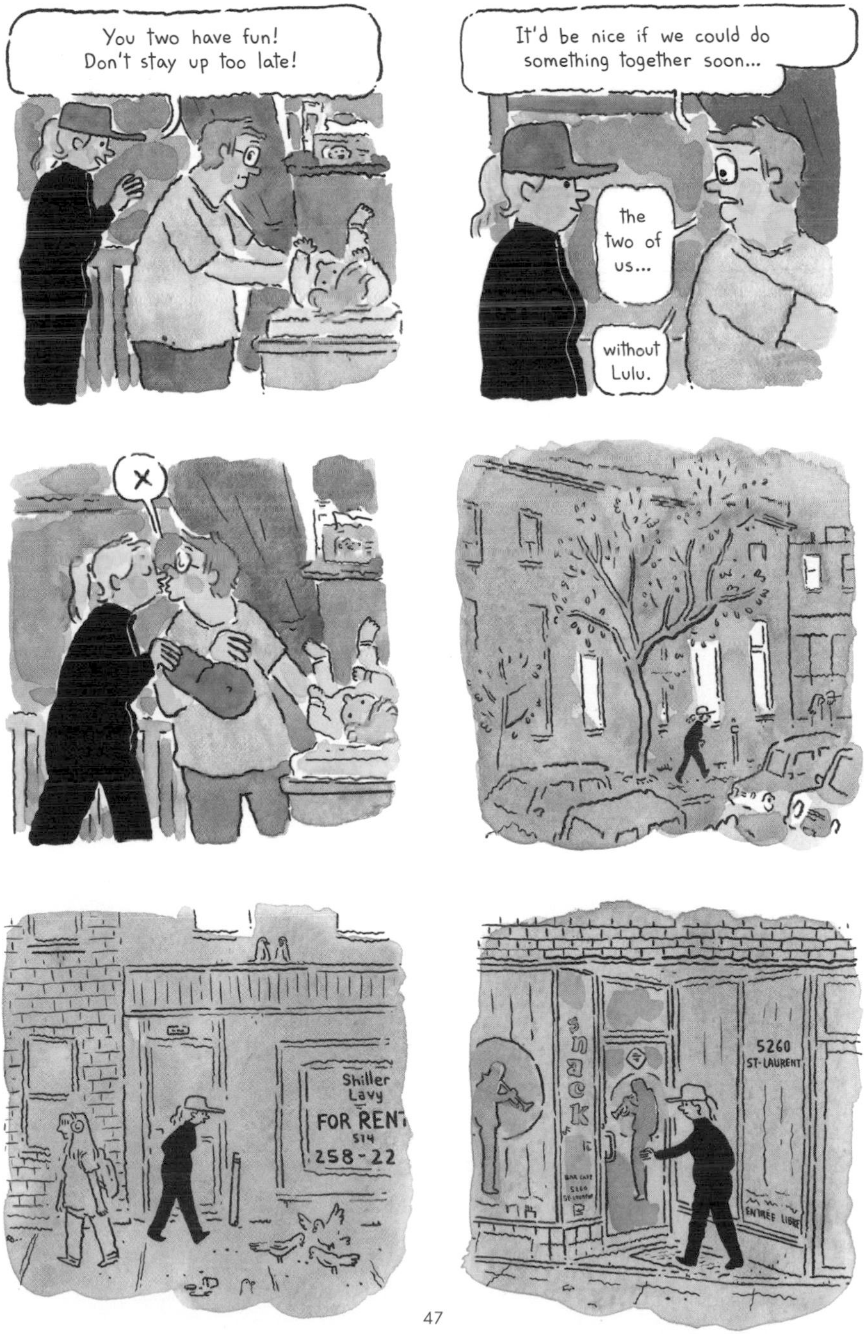
You two have fun!
Don't stay up too late!
It'd be nice if we could do something together soon...
the two of us...
without Lulu.
Shiller
Lavy
FOR RENT
514
258-22
snack
5260
ST-LAURENT

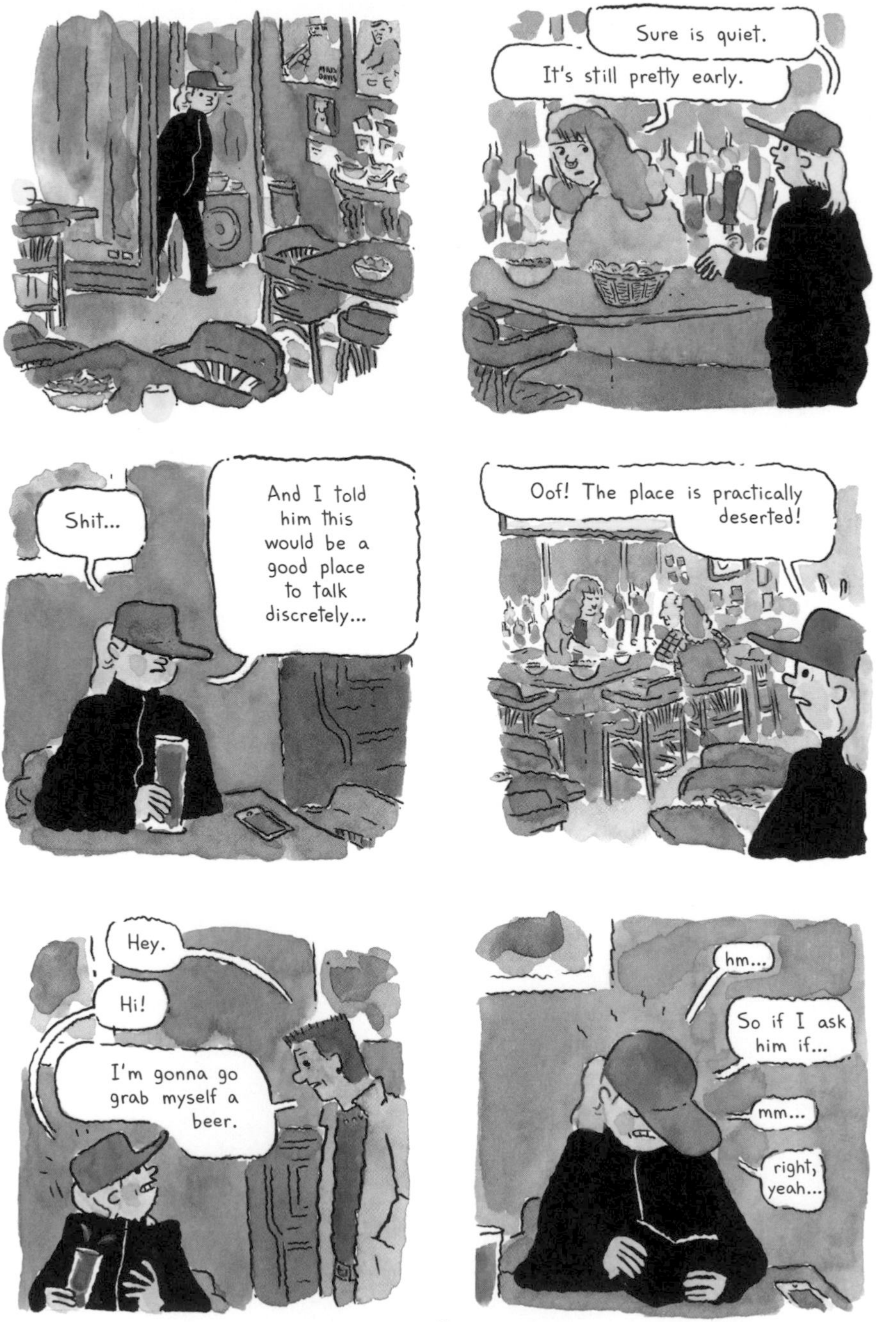
Sure is quiet.
It's still pretty early.
Shit...
And I told him this would be a good place to talk discretely...
Oof! The place is practically deserted!
Hey.
Hi!
I'm gonna go grab myself a beer.
hm...
So if I ask him if...
mm...
right, yeah...

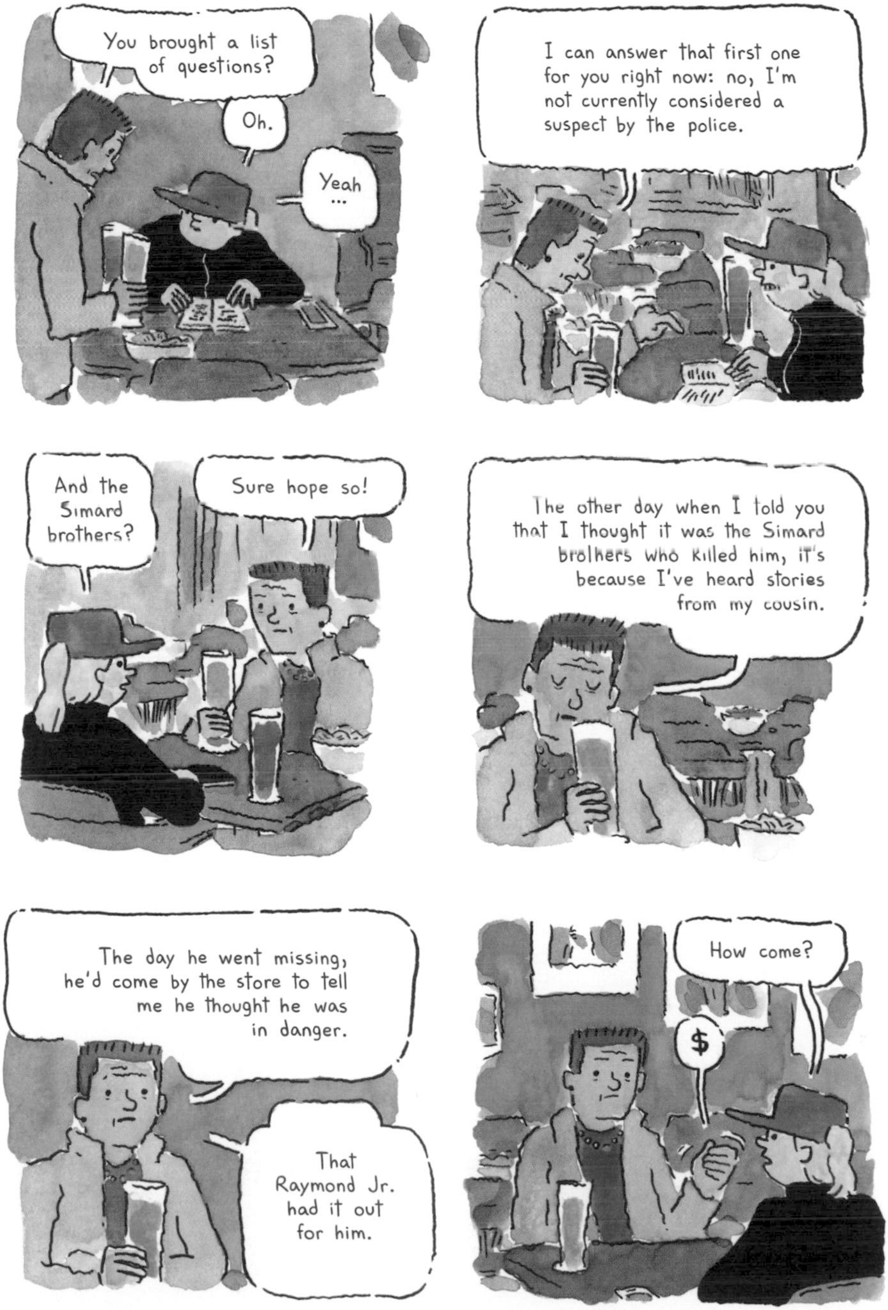
You brought a list of questions?
Oh.
Yeah ...
I can answer that first one for you right now: no, I'm not currently considered a suspect by the police.
And the Simard brothers?
Sure hope so!
The other day when I told you that I thought it was the Simard brothers who killed him, it's because I've heard stories from my cousin.
The day he went missing, he'd come by the store to tell me he thought he was in danger.
That Raymond Jr. had it out for him.
How come?
$

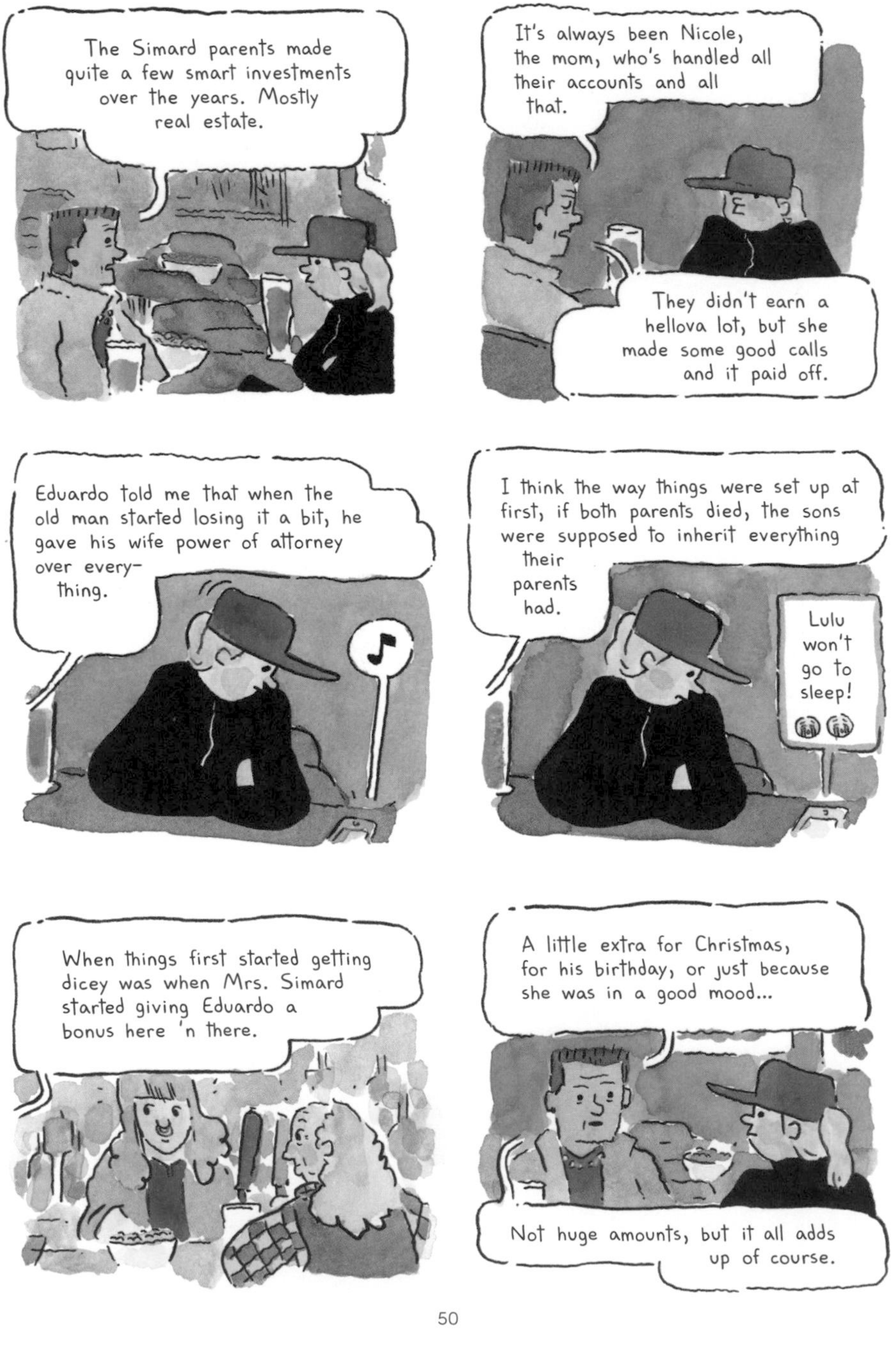
The Simard parents made quite a few smart investments over the years. Mostly real estate.
It's always been Nicole, the mom, who's handled all their accounts and all that.
They didn't earn a hellova lot, but she made some good calls and it paid off.
Eduardo told me that when the old man started losing it a bit, he gave his wife power of attorney over every-thing.
I think the way things were set up at first, if both parents died, the sons were supposed to inherit everything their parents had.
Lulu won't go to sleep!
When things first started getting dicey was when Mrs. Simard started giving Eduardo a bonus here 'n there.
A little extra for Christmas, for his birthday, or just because she was in a good mood...
Not huge amounts, but it all adds up of course.

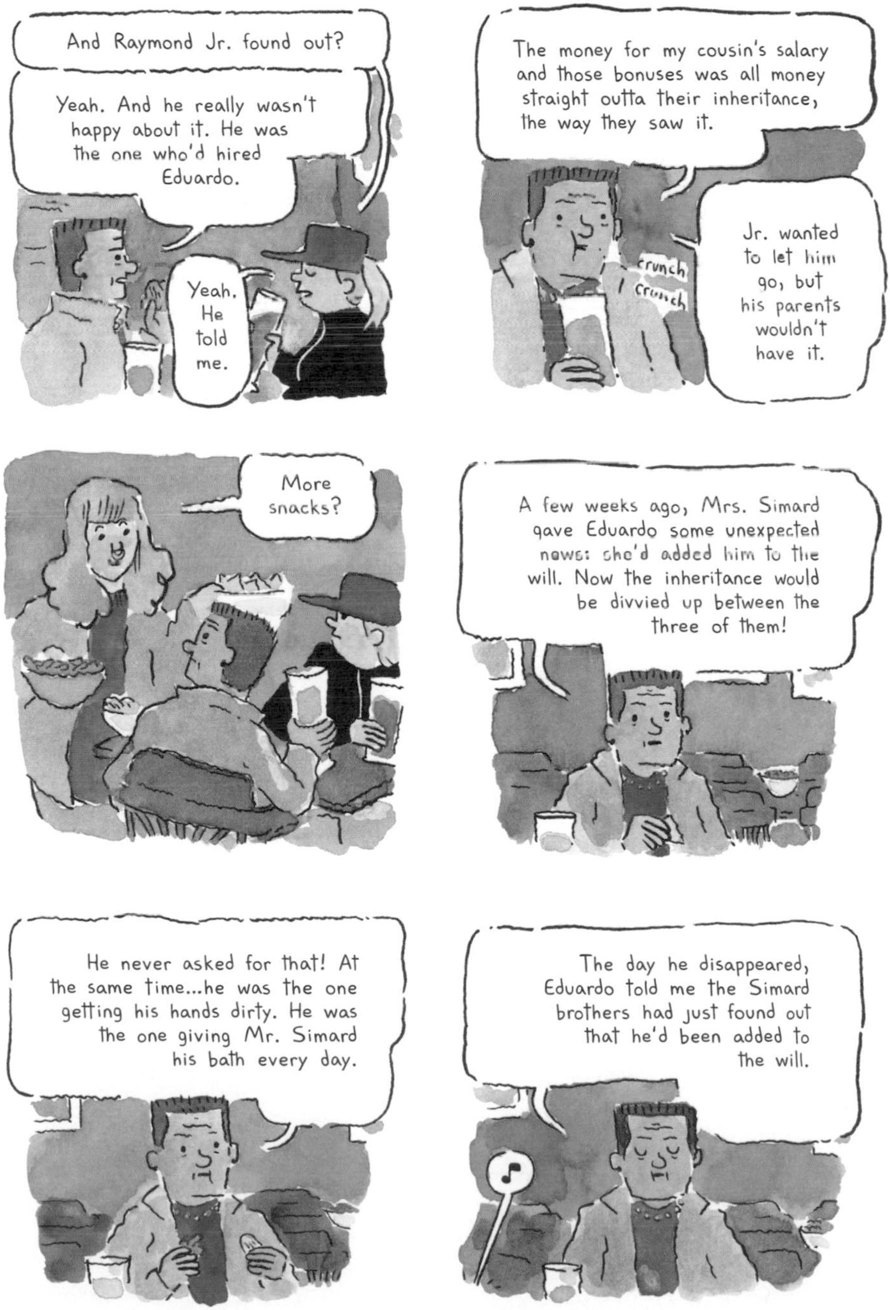

And Raymond Jr. found out?
Yeah. And he really wasn't happy about it. He was the one who'd hired Eduardo.
Yeah. He told me.
The money for my cousin's salary and those bonuses was all money straight outta their inheritance, the way they saw it.
crunch
crunch
Jr. wanted to let him go, but his parents wouldn't have it.
More snacks?
A few weeks ago, Mrs. Simard gave Eduardo some unexpected news: she'd added him to the will. Now the inheritance would be divvied up between the three of them!
He never asked for that! At the same time...he was the one getting his hands dirty. He was the one giving Mr. Simard his bath every day.
The day he disappeared, Eduardo told me the Simard brothers had just found out that he'd been added to the will.

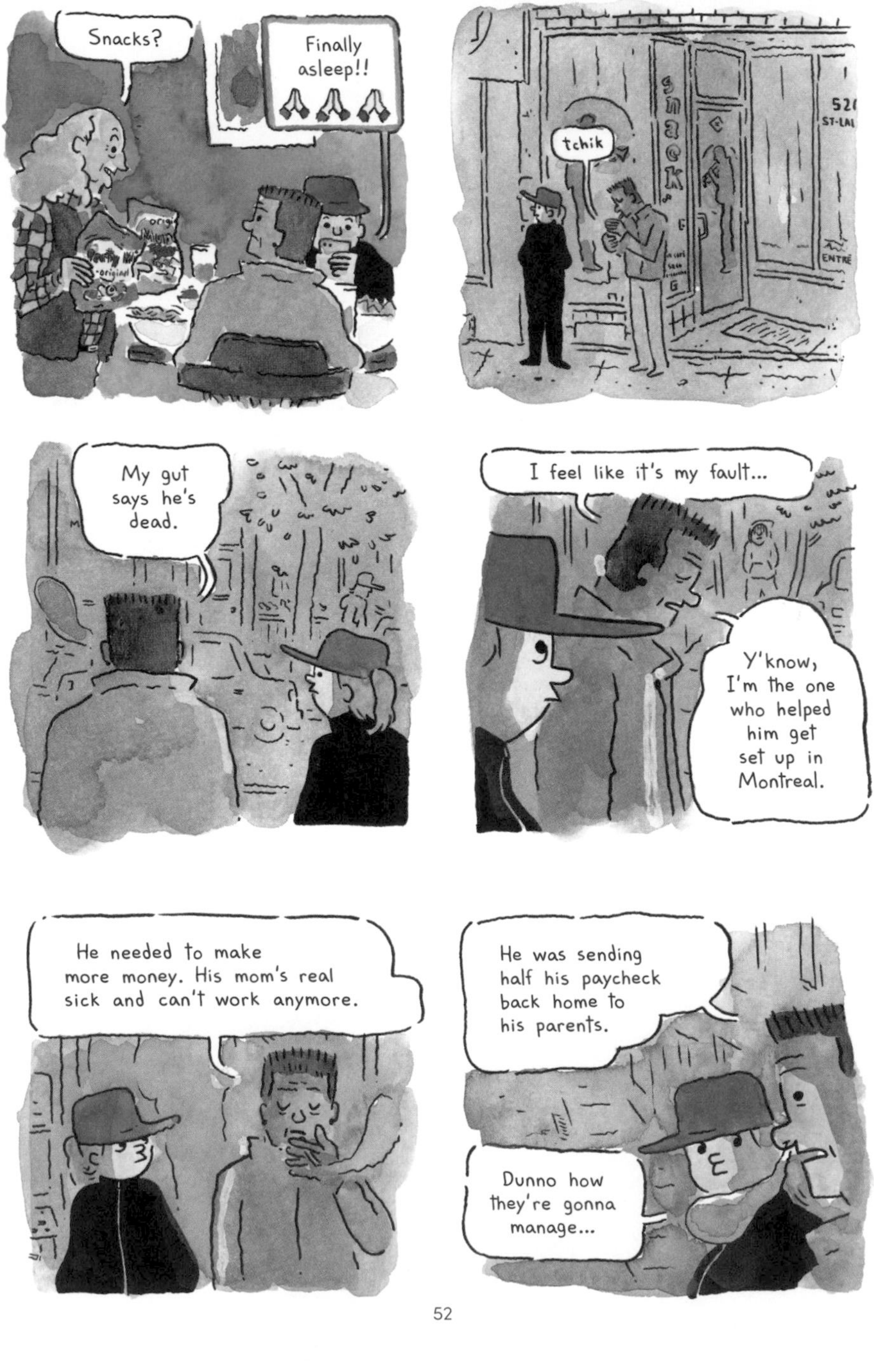
Snacks?
Finally asleep!!
tchik
My gut says he's dead.
I feel like it's my fault...
Y'know, I'm the one who helped him get set up in Montreal.
He needed to make more money. His mom's real sick and can't work anymore.
He was sending half his paycheck back home to his parents.
Dunno how they're gonna manage...

Secretly, he was really glad they'd added him to the will. But he'd never have said as much.

RRR

wWAAᴀ mmf

WAH! Rd

I've got two suspects. A serious motive.

Ah Ah

Mf...

I need to find Lionel Simard... ...and the body.

Without the body they're home free.

gloop

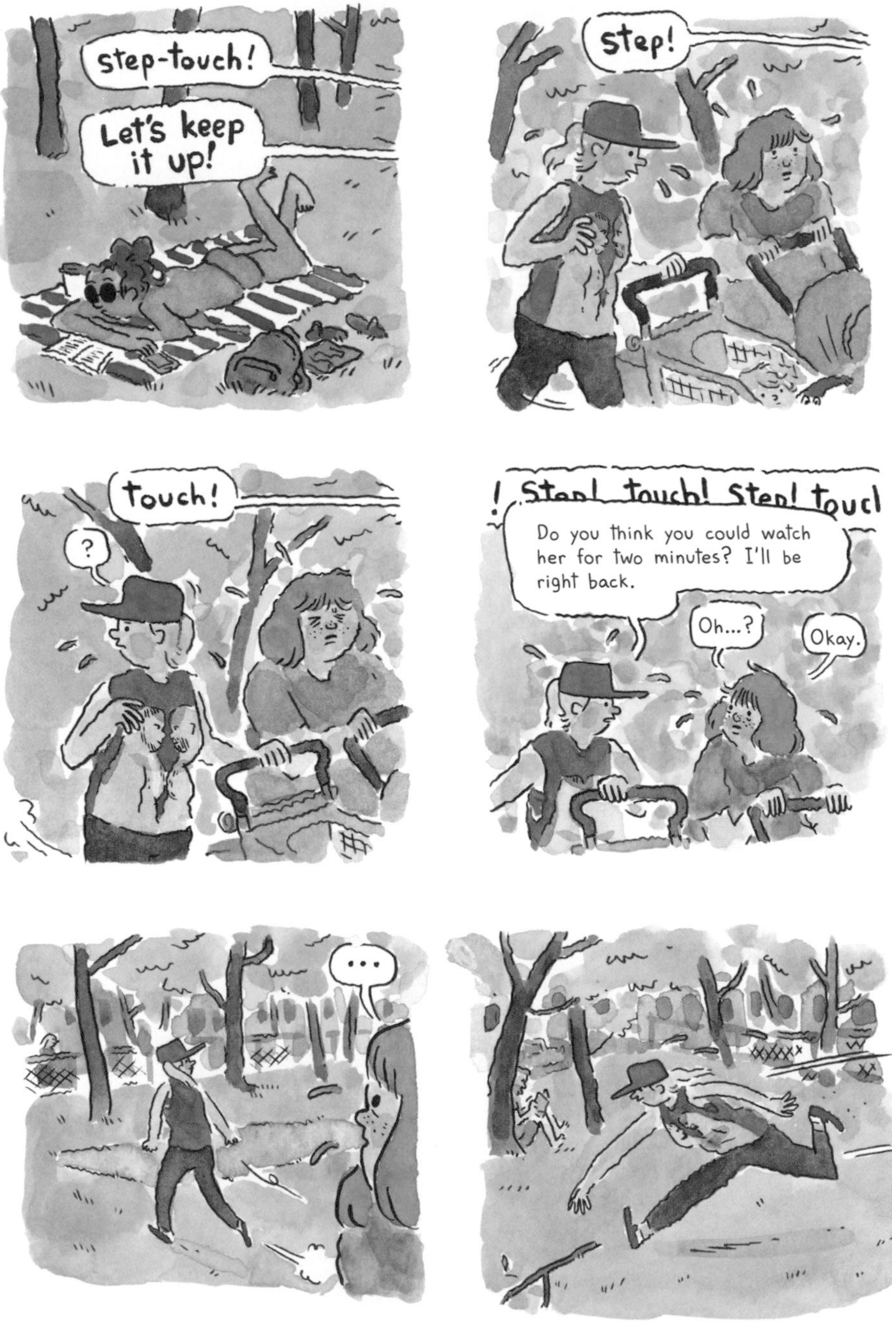
step-touch!
Let's keep it up!
step!
touch!
?
Step! touch! Step!
Do you think you could watch her for two minutes? I'll be right back.
Oh...?
Okay.
...

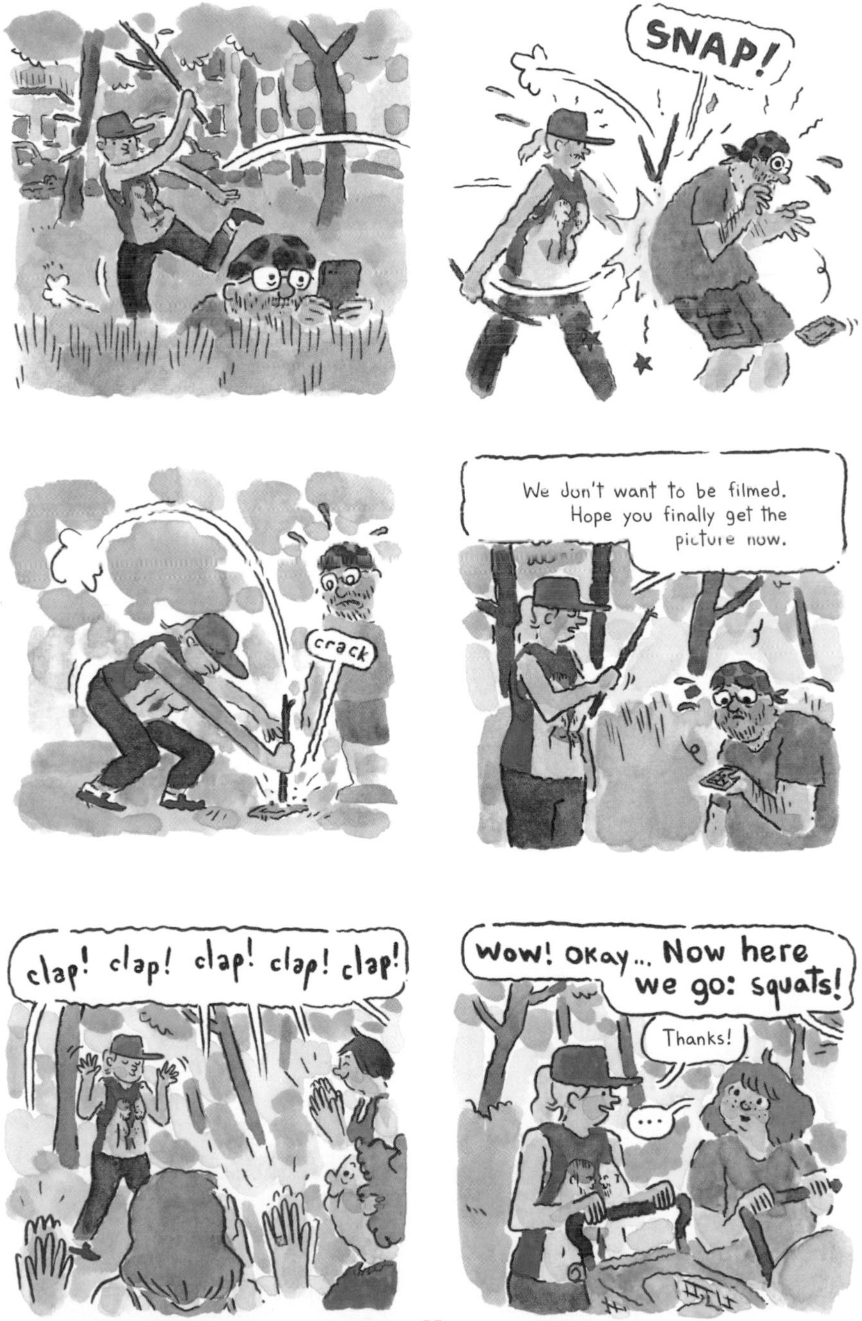
SNAP!
crack
We don't want to be filmed. Hope you finally get the picture now.
clap! clap! clap! clap! clap!
Wow! Okay... Now here we go: squats!
Thanks!
...

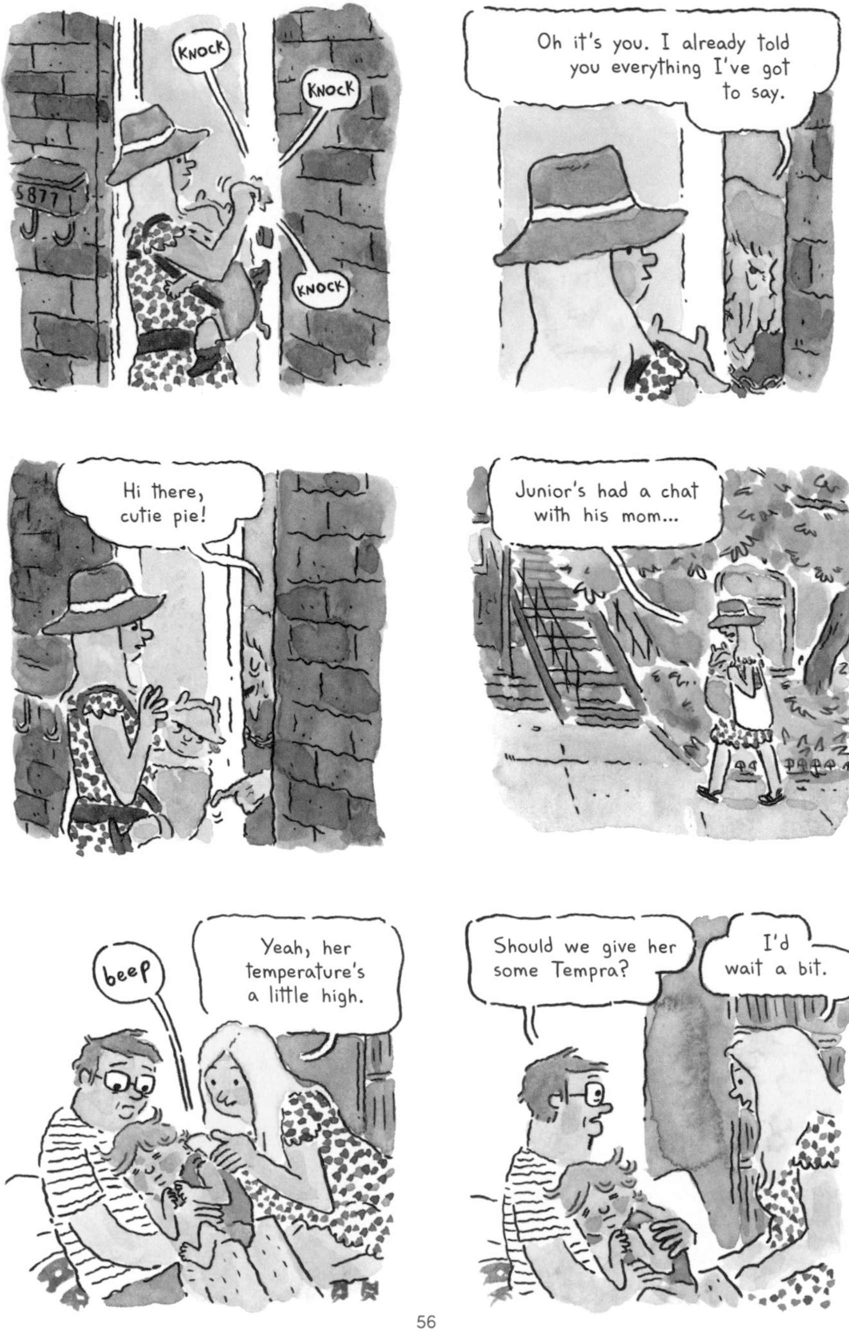
5877
KNOCK
KNOCK
KNOCK
Oh it's you. I already told you everything I've got to say.
Hi there, cutie pie!
Junior's had a chat with his mom...
beep
Yeah, her temperature's a little high.
Should we give her some Tempra?
I'd wait a bit.

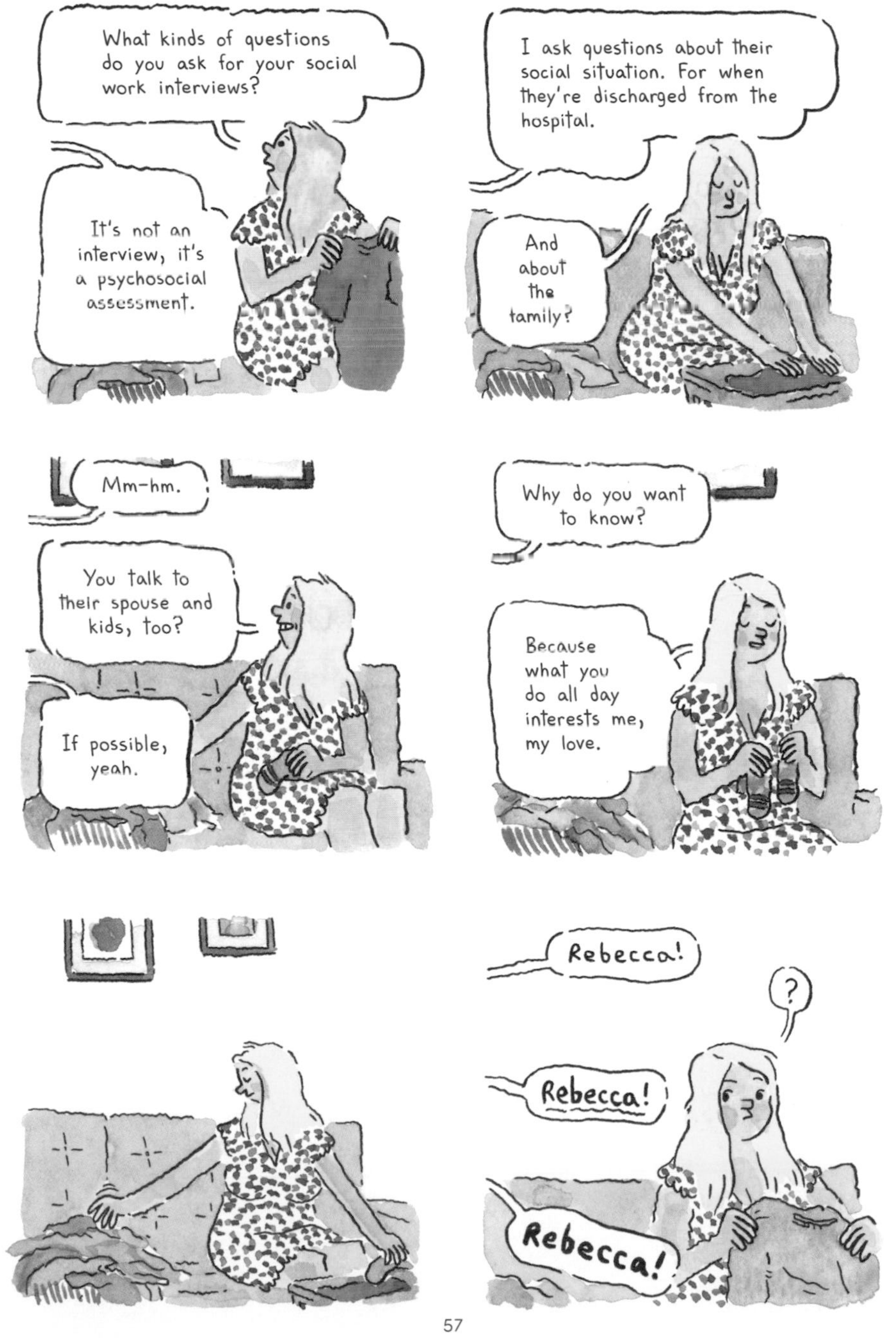
What kinds of questions do you ask for your social work interviews?
It's not an interview, it's a psychosocial assessment.
I ask questions about their social situation. For when they're discharged from the hospital.
And about the family?
Mm-hm.
You talk to their spouse and kids, too?
If possible, yeah.
Why do you want to know?
Because what you do all day interests me, my love.
Rebecca!
?
Rebecca!
Rebecca!

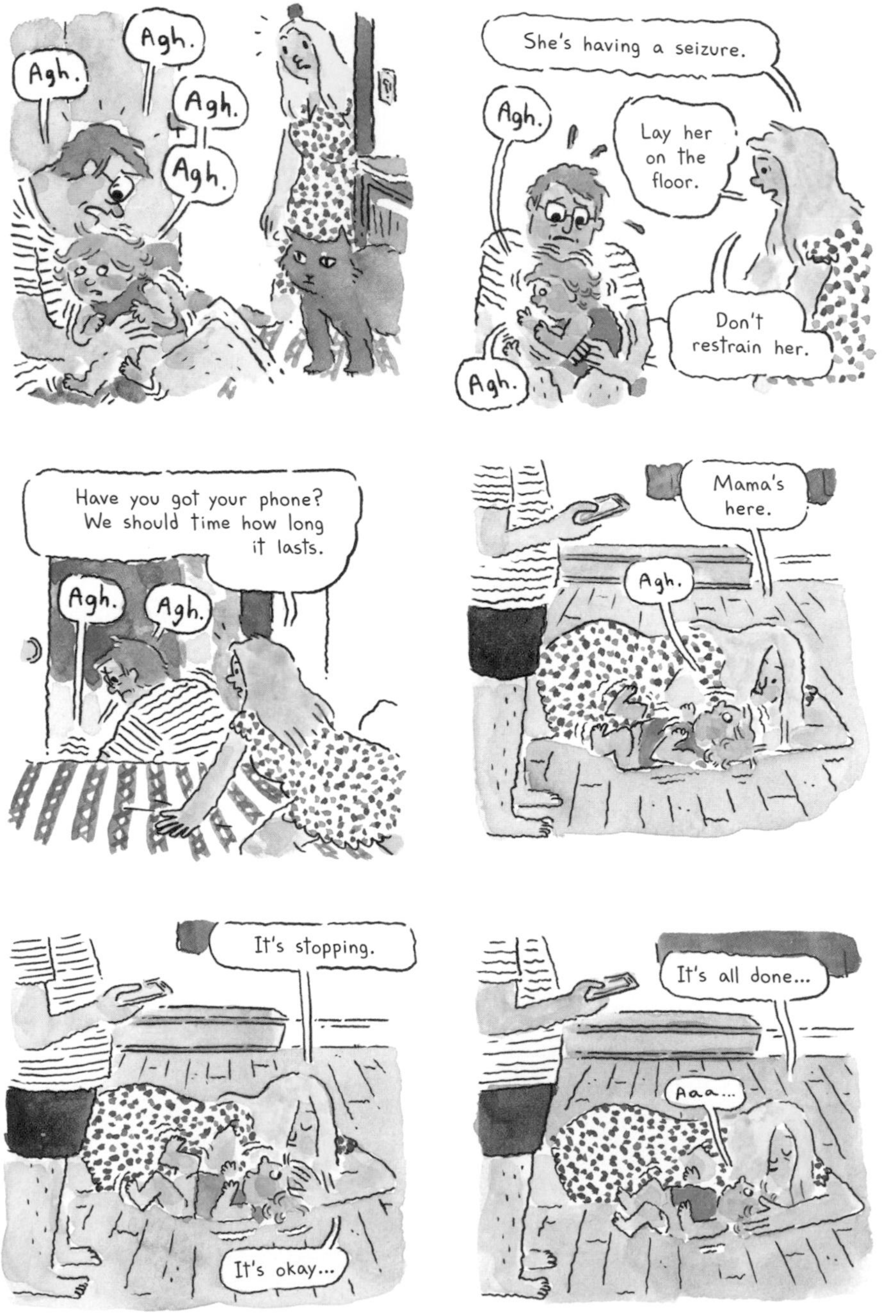
Agh.
Agh.
Agh.
Agh.
She's having a seizure.
Agh.
Lay her on the floor.
Agh.
Don't restrain her.
Have you got your phone? We should time how long it lasts.
Agh.
Agh.
Mama's here.
Agh.
It's stopping.
It's okay...
It's all done...
Aaa...

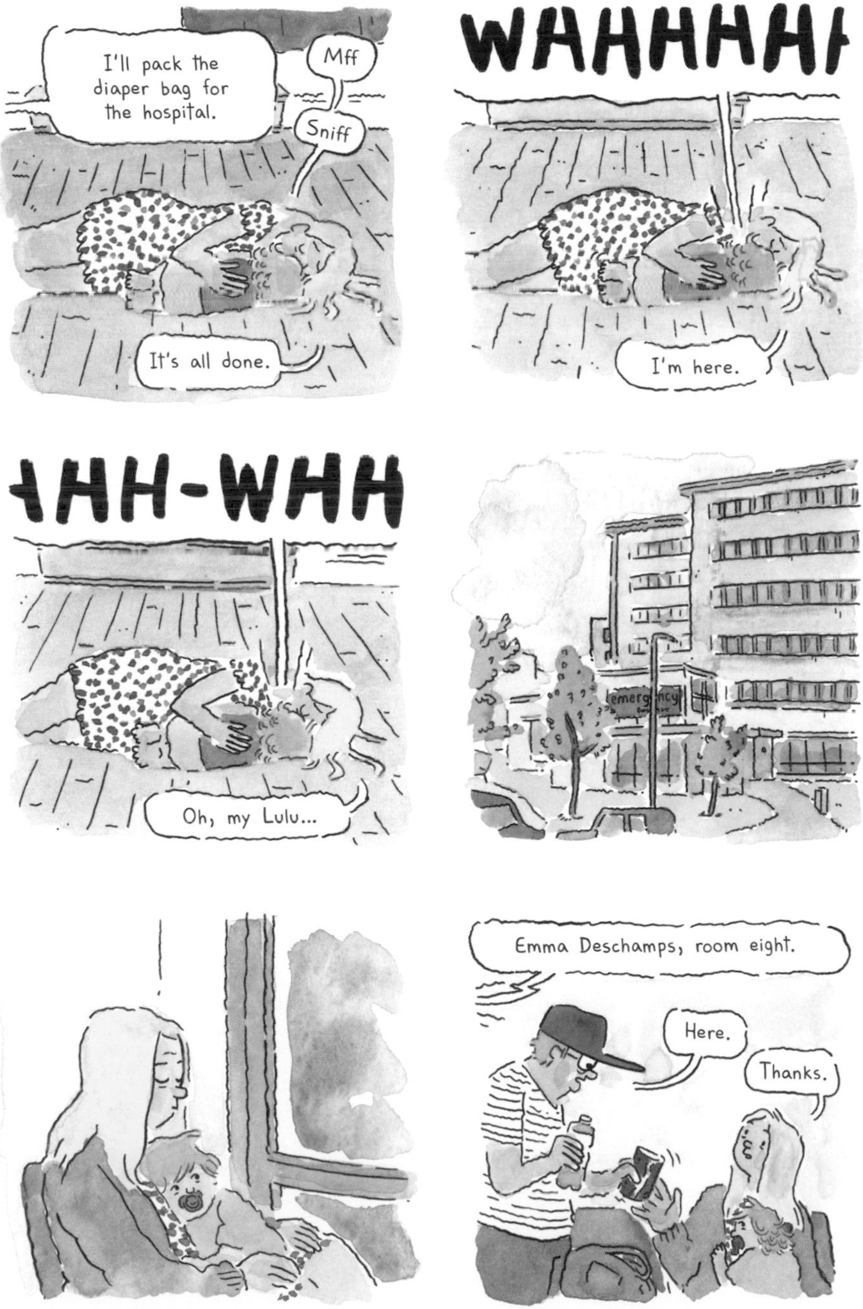
I'll pack the diaper bag for the hospital.
Mff
Sniff
It's all done.
WAHHHH
I'm here.
HH-WHH
Oh, my Lulu...
Emma Deschamps, room eight.
Here.
Thanks.

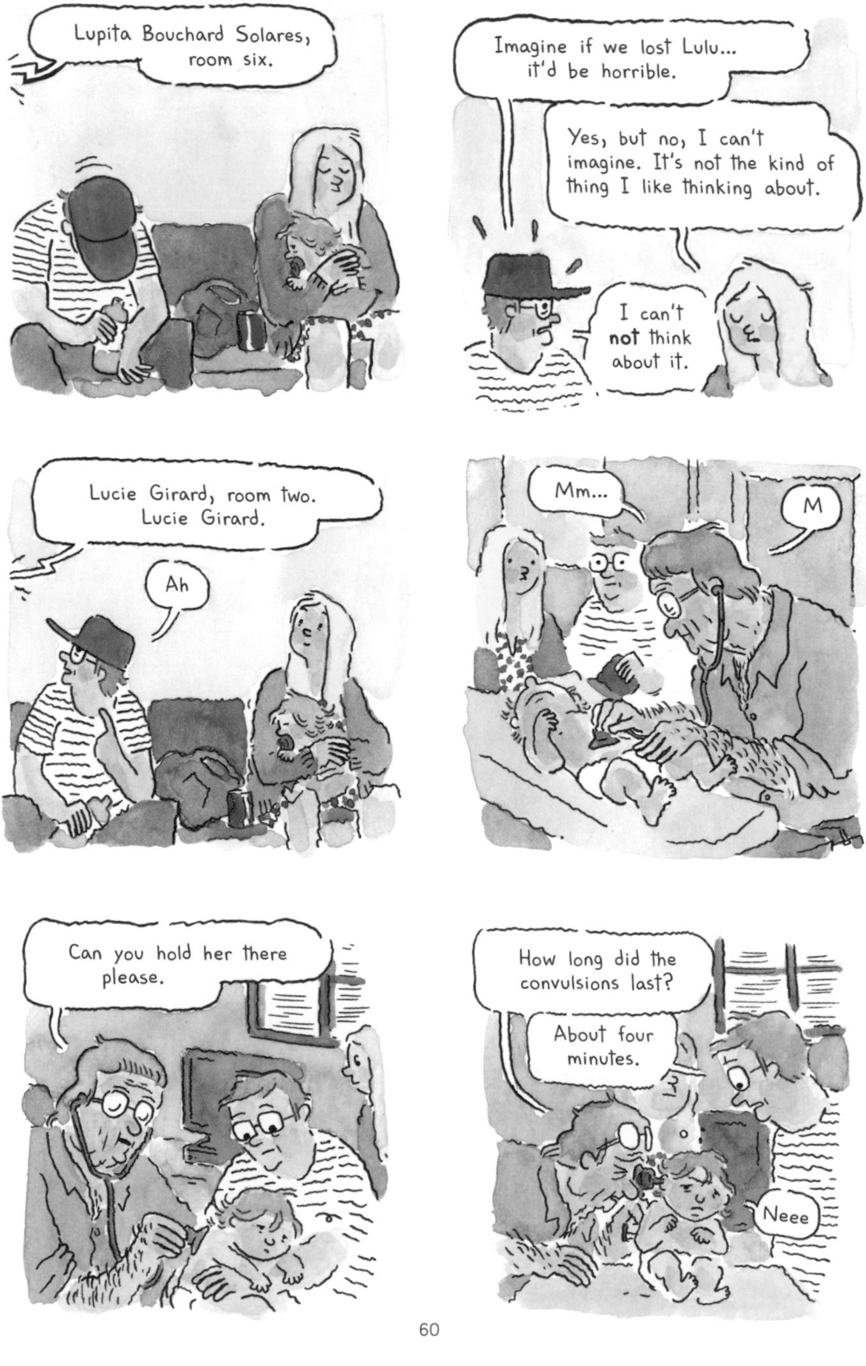
Lupita Bouchard Solares, room six.
Imagine if we lost Lulu... it'd be horrible.
Yes, but no, I can't imagine. It's not the kind of thing I like thinking about.
I can't **not** think about it.
Lucie Girard, room two. Lucie Girard.
Ah
Mm...
M
Can you hold her there please.
How long did the convulsions last?
About four minutes.
Neee

An eternity in other words.

Definitely!

You can rest assured, nothing at all to worry about.

It was a febrile seizure. It can happen sometimes in young children when a fever goes up very quickly. Come her wedding day, she won't have the vaguest memory of it! I guarantee it!

I prescribe some rest.

Hehehe!

Did you notice how the doctor looked exactly like you?

What?! He didn't at all.

I think I'm going to take a run while she's sleeping.

Yeah!

Good plan! Go-go!

Pascal GIRARD
Travailleur
Social Worker

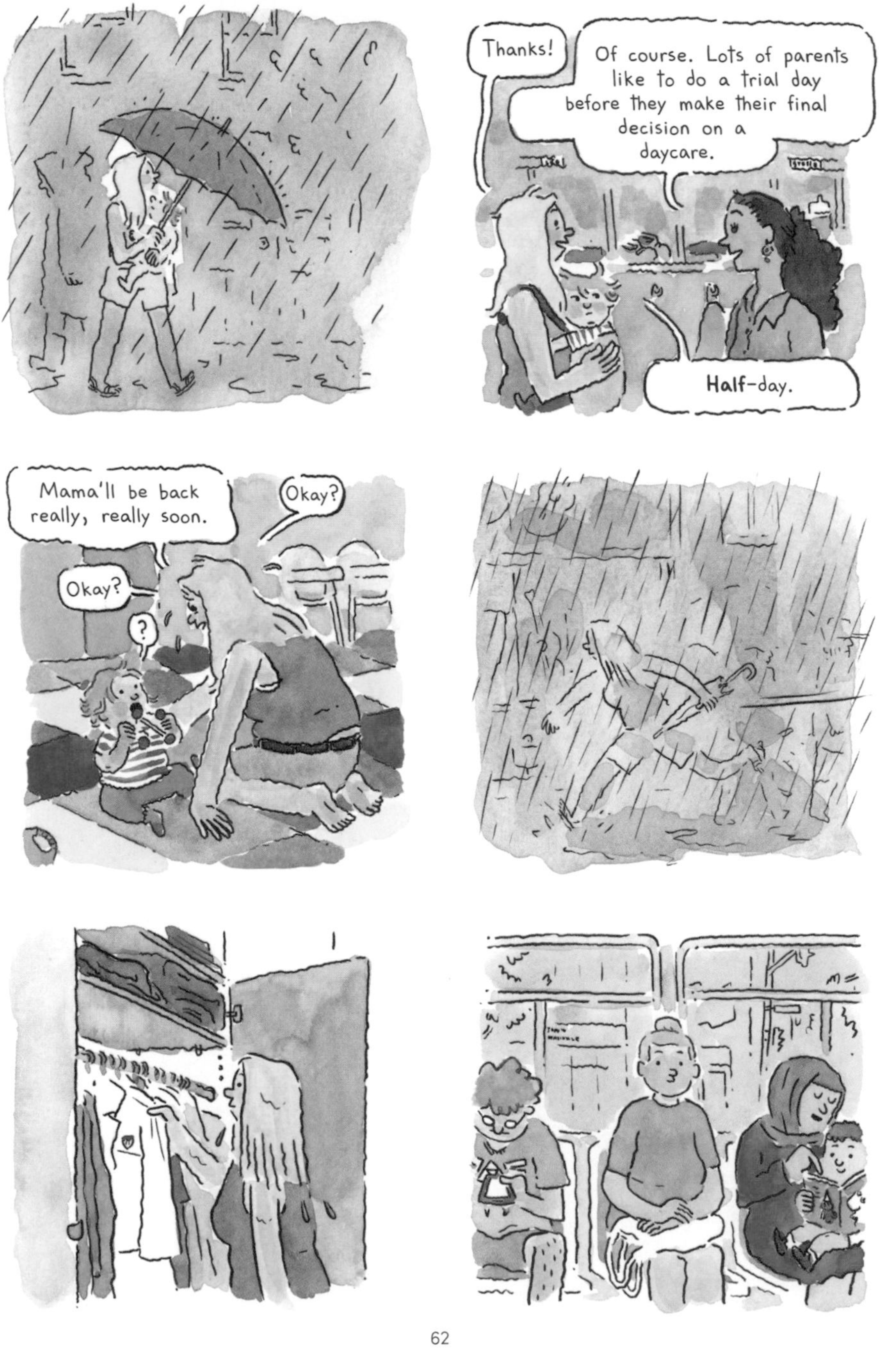
Thanks!
Of course. Lots of parents like to do a trial day before they make their final decision on a daycare.
Half-day.
Mama'll be back really, really soon.
Okay?
Okay?
?

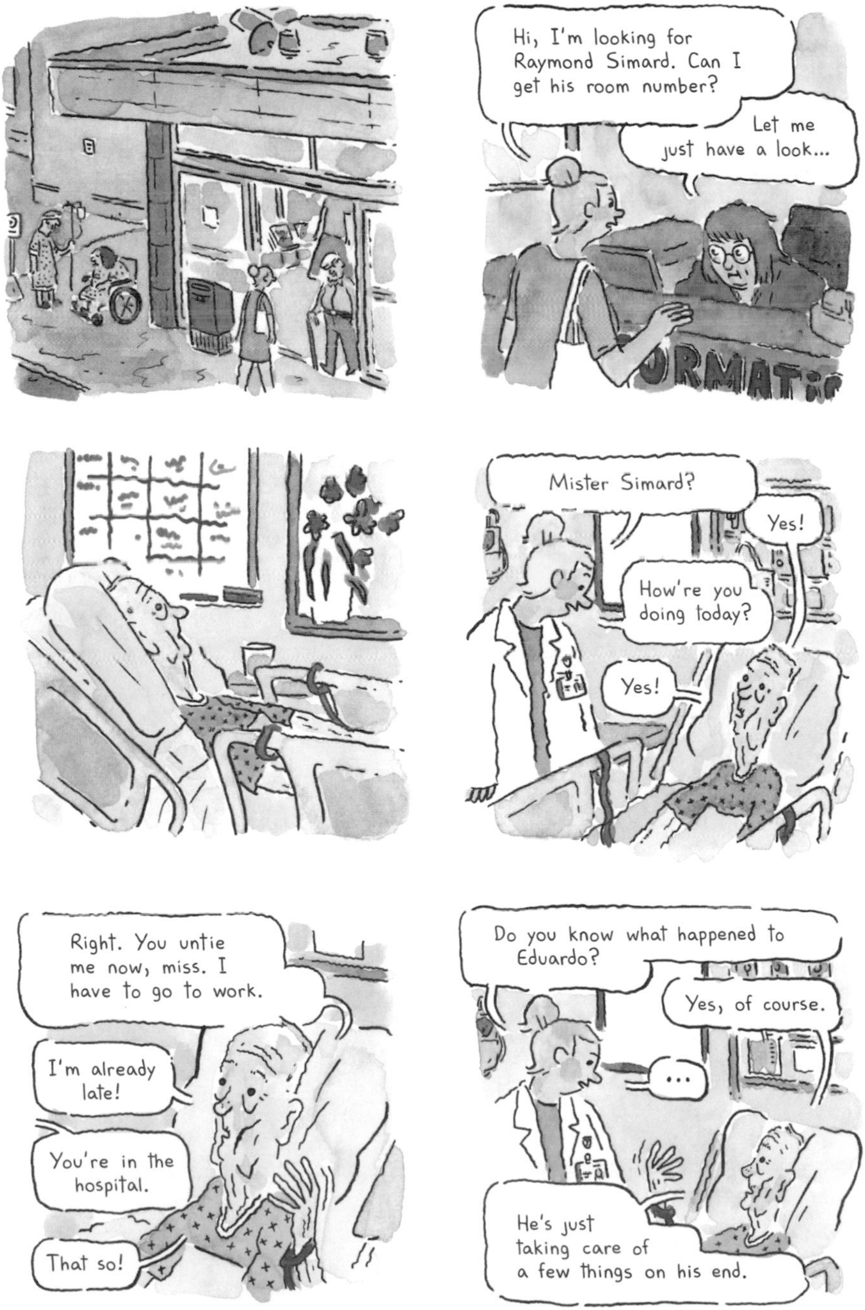
Hi, I'm looking for Raymond Simard. Can I get his room number?
Let me just have a look...
ORMATI
Mister Simard?
Yes!
How're you doing today?
Yes!
Right. You untie me now, miss. I have to go to work.
I'm already late!
You're in the hospital.
That so!
Do you know what happened to Eduardo?
Yes, of course.
...
He's just taking care of a few things on his end.

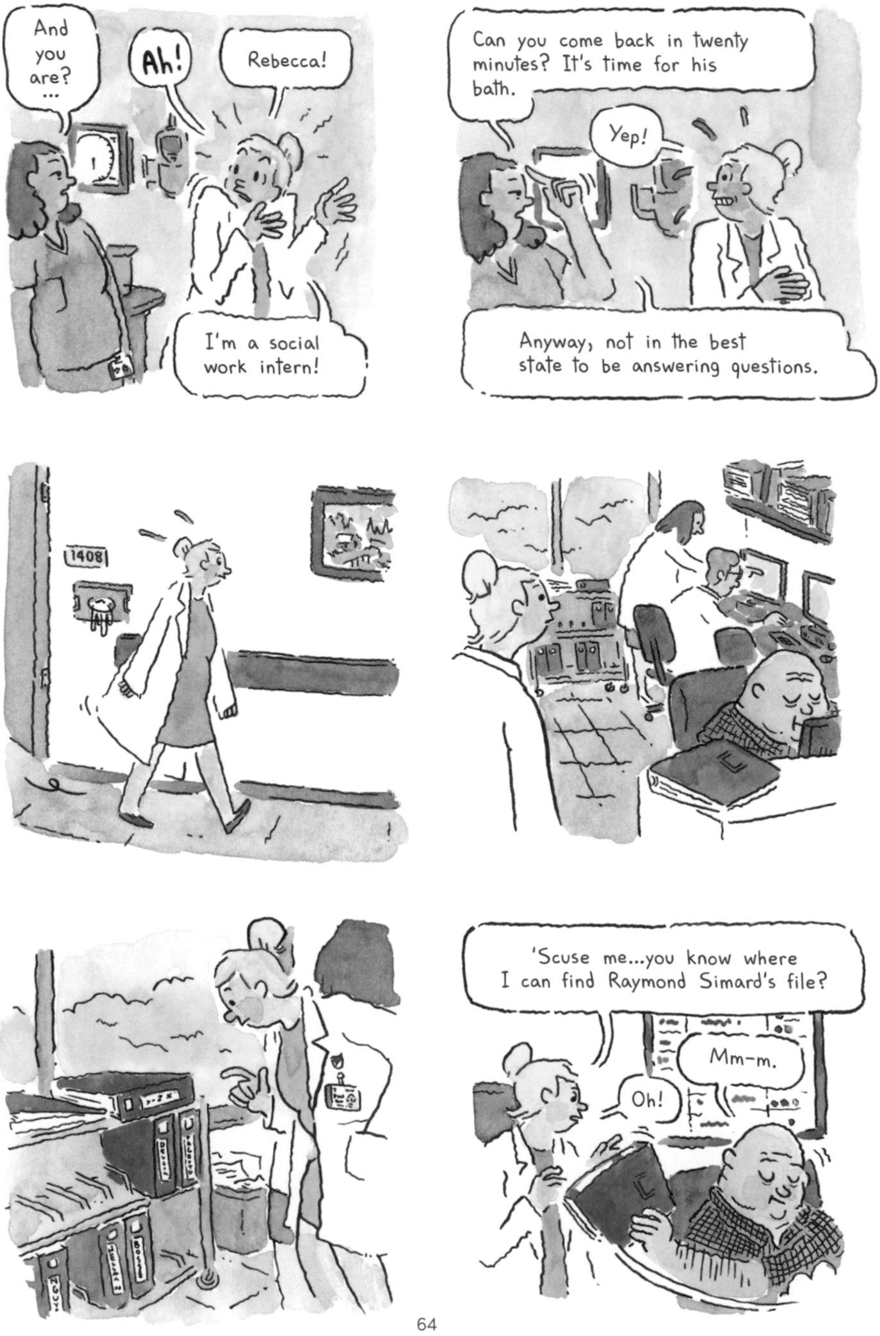
And you are? ...
Ah!
Rebecca!
I'm a social work intern!
Can you come back in twenty minutes? It's time for his bath.
Yep!
Anyway, not in the best state to be answering questions.
1408
'Scuse me...you know where I can find Raymond Simard's file?
Oh!
Mm-m.

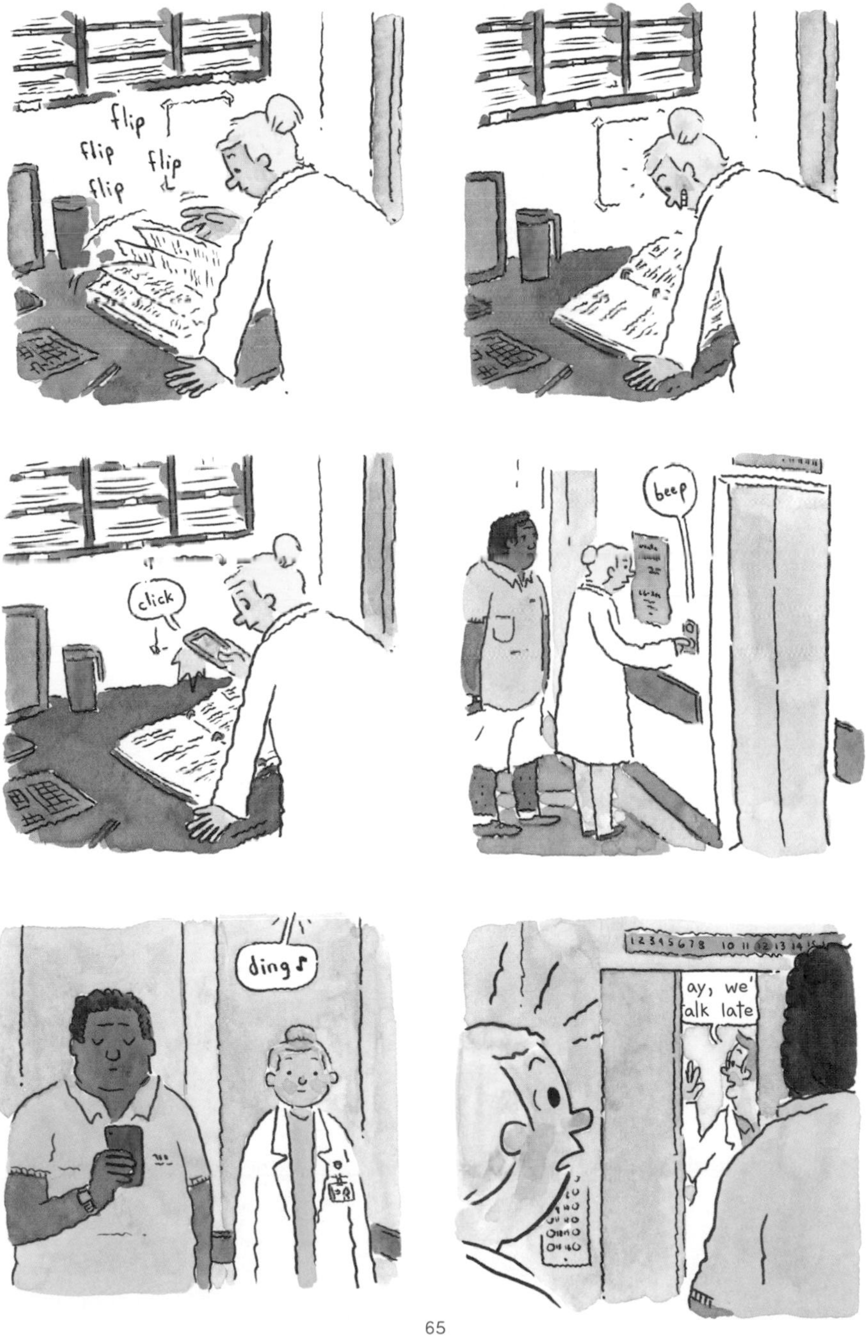
flip
flip
flip
flip
click
beep
ding♪
1 2 3 4 5 6 7 8 10 11 12 13 14
ay, we'
alk late

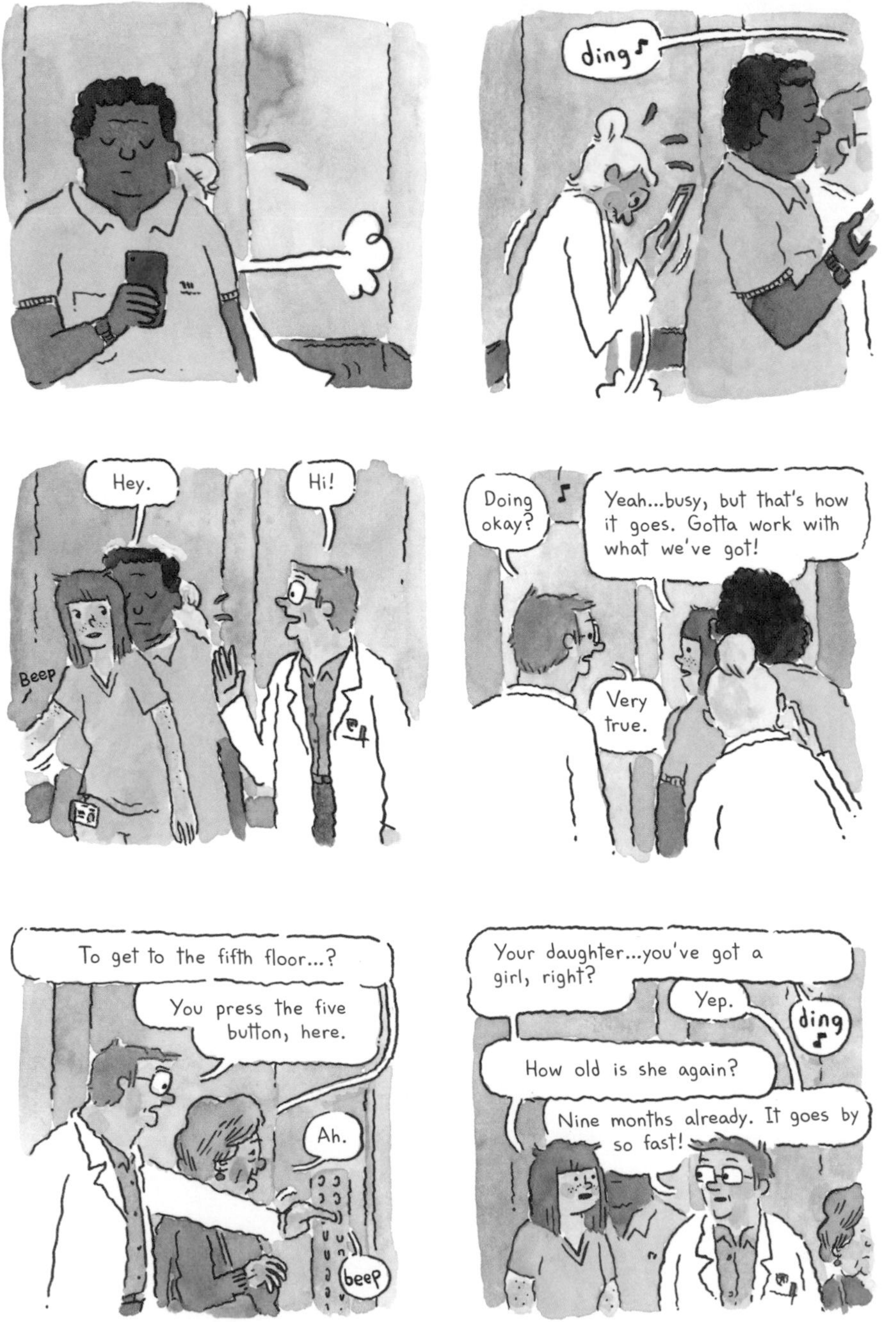
ding
Hey.
Hi!
Beep
Doing okay?
Yeah...busy, but that's how it goes. Gotta work with what we've got!
Very true.
To get to the fifth floor...?
You press the five button, here.
Ah.
beep
Your daughter...you've got a girl, right?
Yep.
ding
How old is she again?
Nine months already. It goes by so fast!

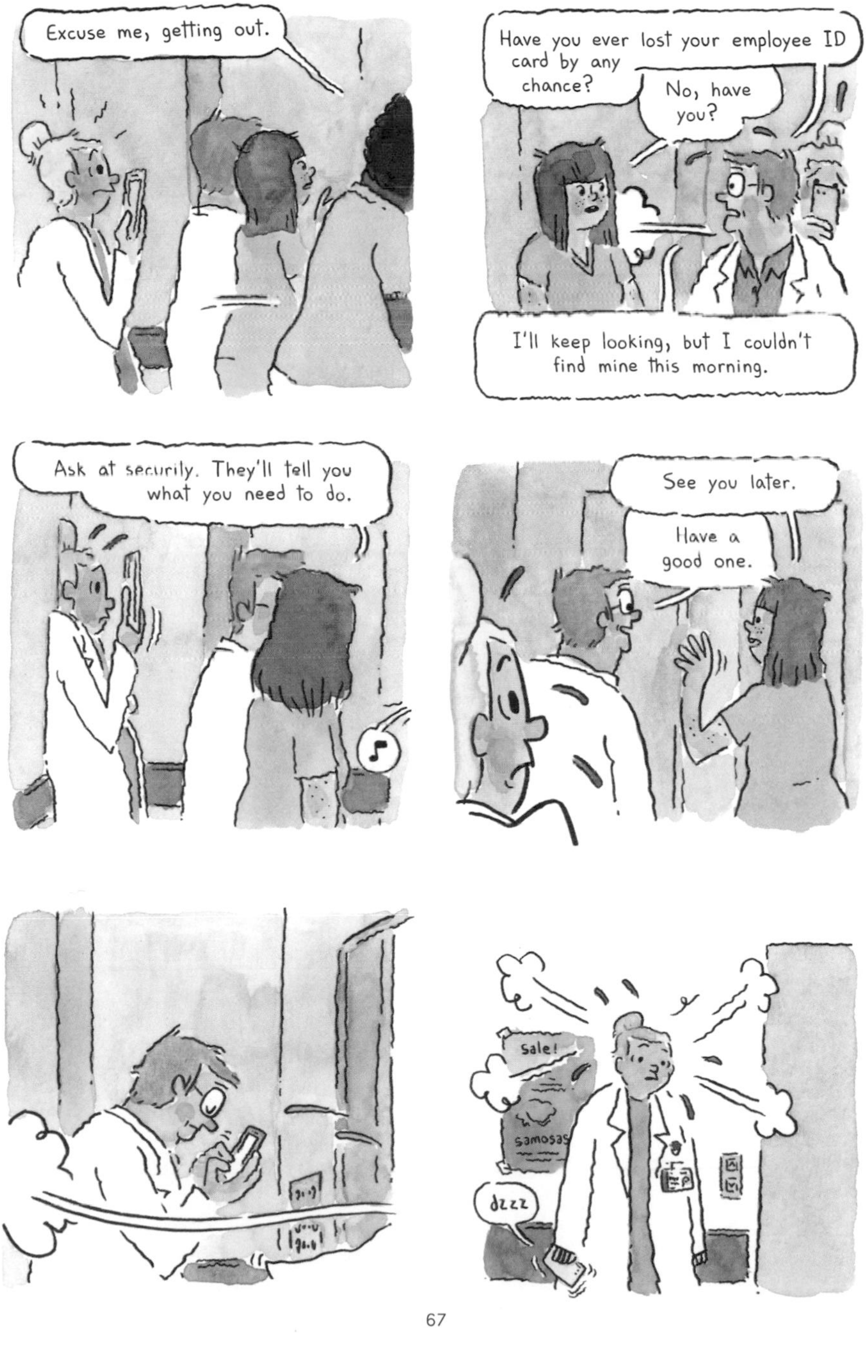
Excuse me, getting out.
Have you ever lost your employee ID card by any chance?
No, have you?
I'll keep looking, but I couldn't find mine this morning.
Ask at security. They'll tell you what you need to do.
See you later.
Have a good one.
Sale!
samosas
dzzz

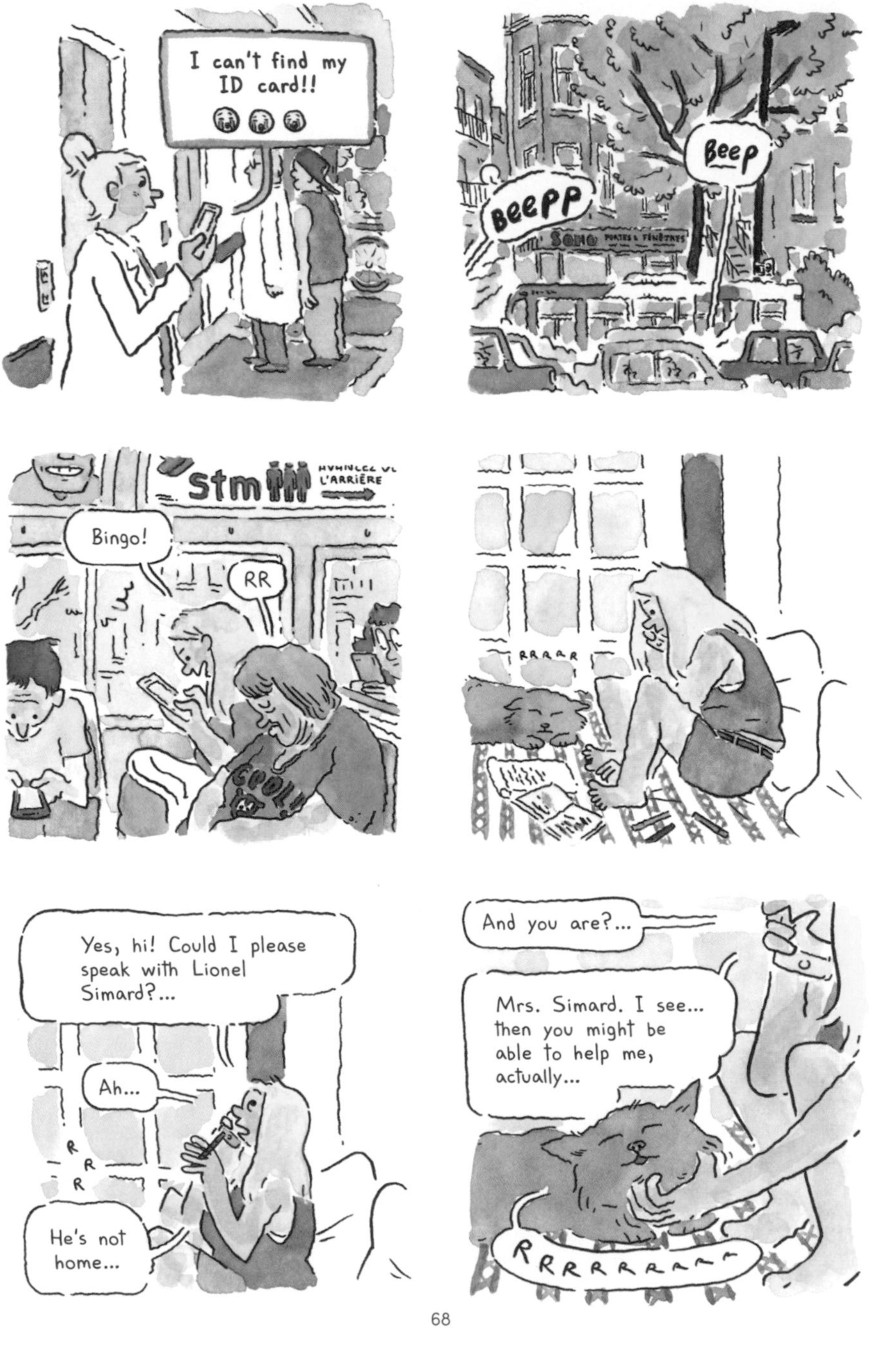
I can't find my ID card!!
BEEPP
Beep
stm
L'ARRIÈRE
Bingo!
RR
COOL!
RRRRR
Yes, hi! Could I please speak with Lionel Simard?...
Ah...
R
R
R
He's not home...
And you are?...
Mrs. Simard. I see... then you might be able to help me, actually...
RRRRRRRRR

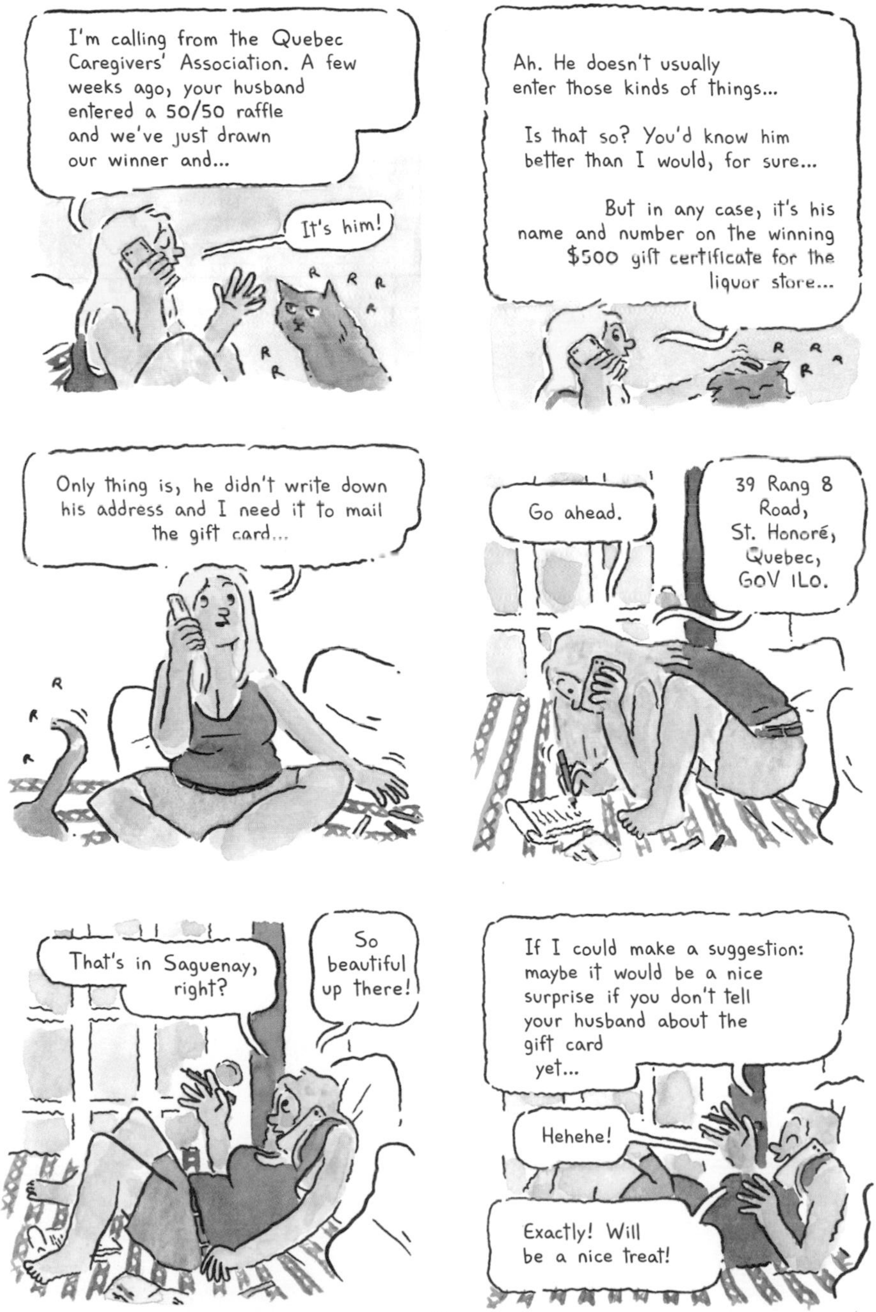
I'm calling from the Quebec Caregivers' Association. A few weeks ago, your husband entered a 50/50 raffle and we've just drawn our winner and...
It's him!
R R R R R R
Ah. He doesn't usually enter those kinds of things...
Is that so? You'd know him better than I would, for sure...
But in any case, it's his name and number on the winning $500 gift certificate for the liquor store...
R R R R
Only thing is, he didn't write down his address and I need it to mail the gift card...
R R R
Go ahead.
39 Rang 8 Road, St. Honoré, Quebec, G0V 1L0.
That's in Saguenay, right?
So beautiful up there!
If I could make a suggestion: maybe it would be a nice surprise if you don't tell your husband about the gift card yet...
Hehehe!
Exactly! Will be a nice treat!

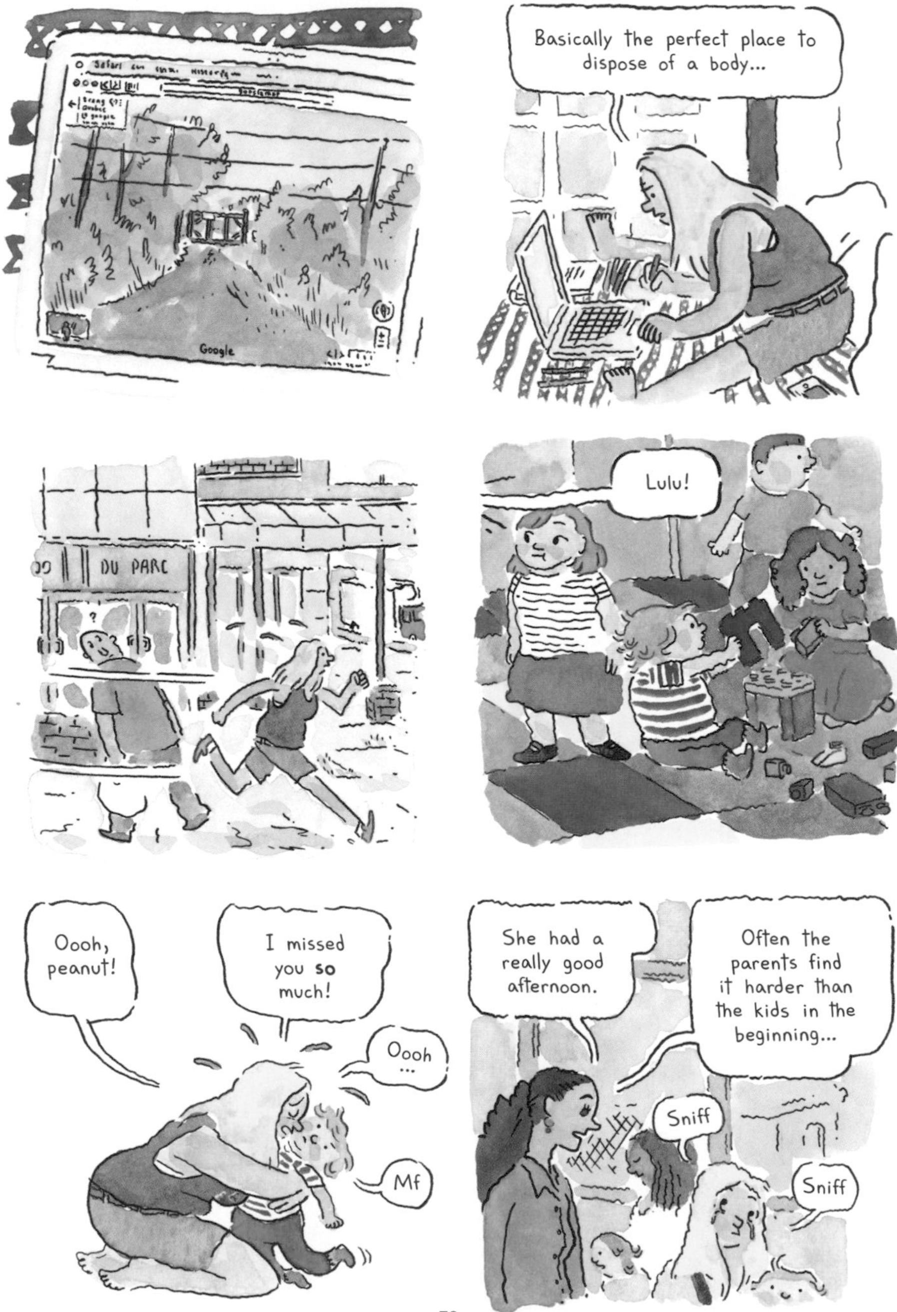
Google
Basically the perfect place to dispose of a body...
DU PARC
Lulu!
Oooh, peanut!
I missed you **so** much!
Oooh ...
Mf
She had a really good afternoon.
Often the parents find it harder than the kids in the beginning...
Sniff
Sniff

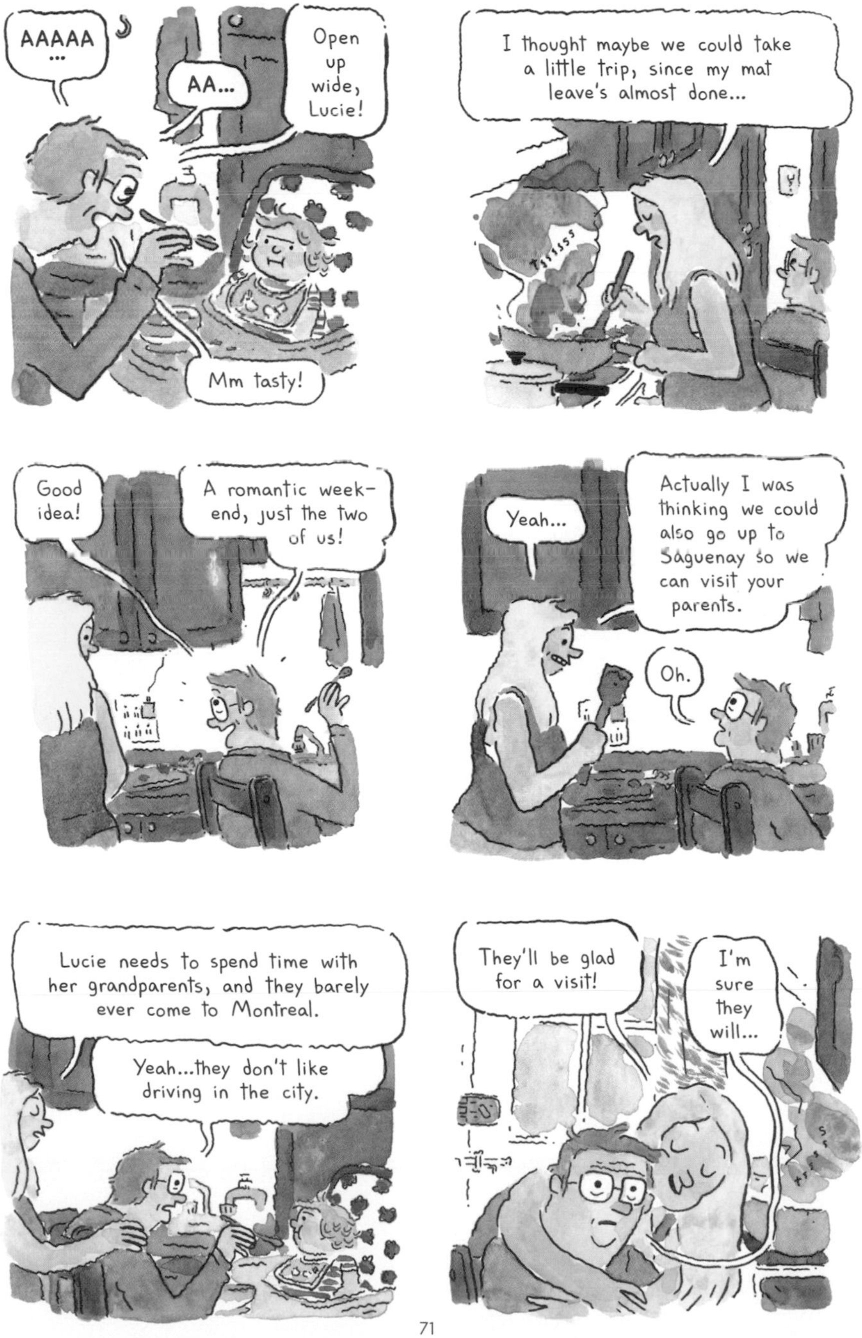
AAAAA
...
AA...
Open up wide, Lucie!
Mm tasty!
I thought maybe we could take a little trip, since my mat leave's almost done...
Good idea!
A romantic week-end, just the two of us!
Yeah...
Actually I was thinking we could also go up to Saguenay so we can visit your parents.
Oh.
Lucie needs to spend time with her grandparents, and they barely ever come to Montreal.
Yeah...they don't like driving in the city.
They'll be glad for a visit!
I'm sure they will...

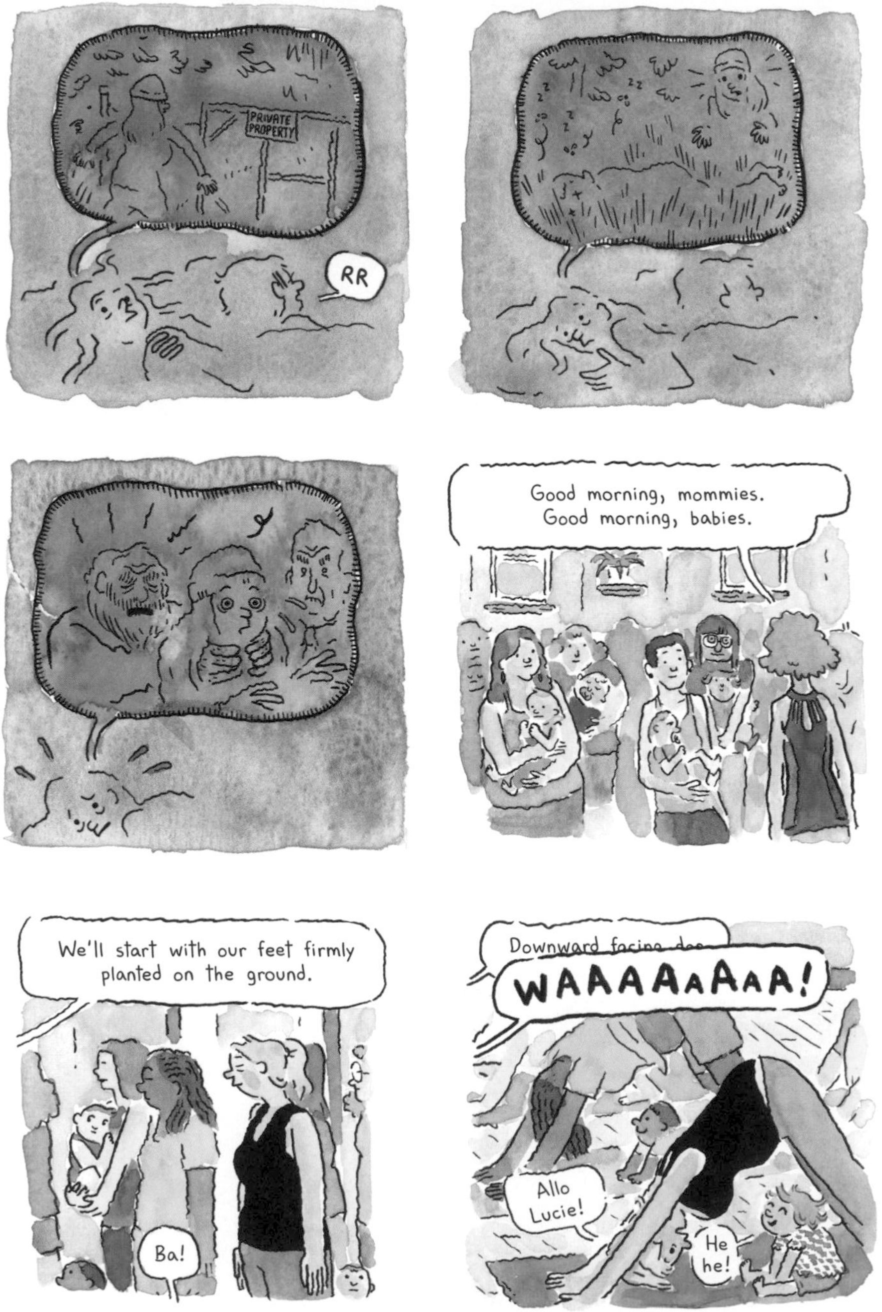
PRIVATE PROPERTY
RR
Good morning, mommies. Good morning, babies.
We'll start with our feet firmly planted on the ground.
Ba!
Downward
WAAAAAAAA!
Allo Lucie!
He he!

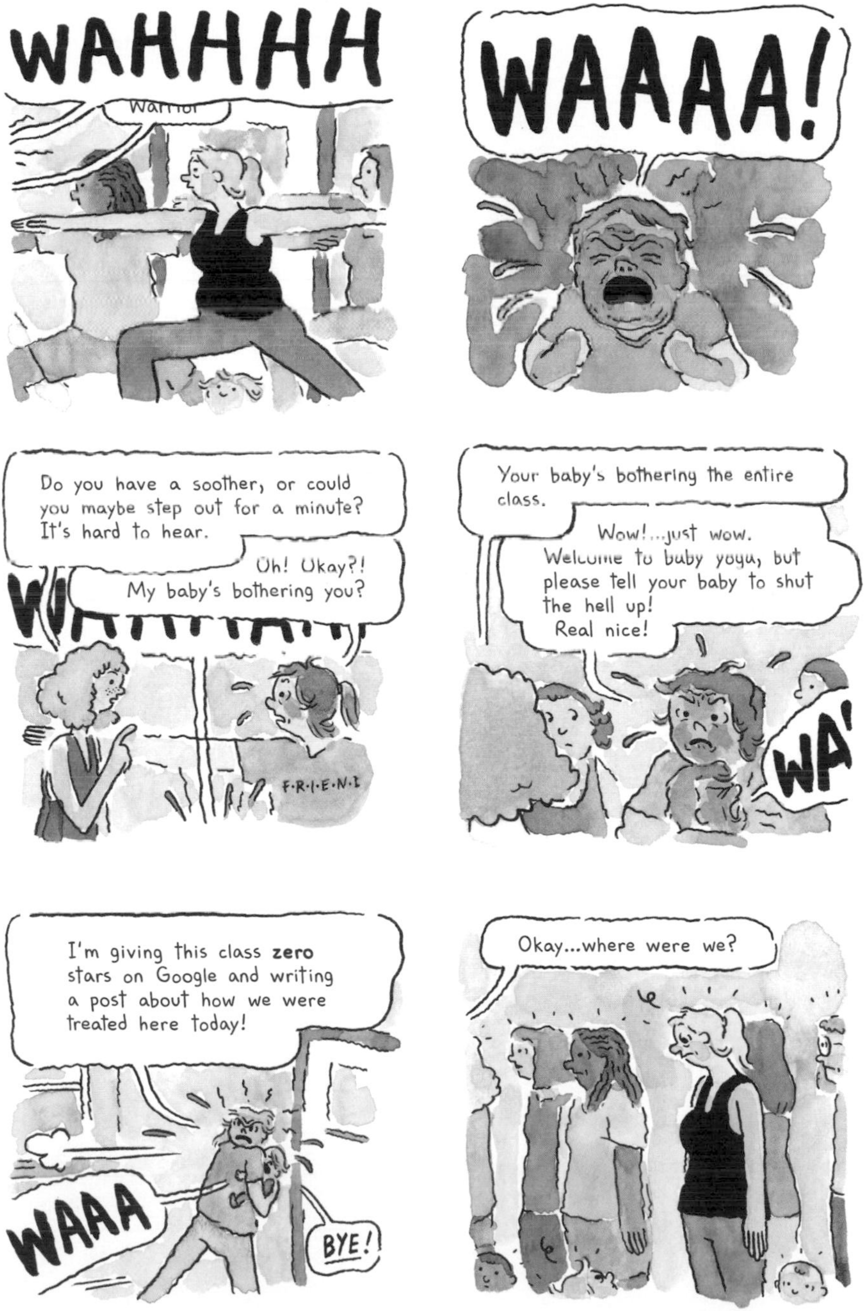
WAHHHH
WAAAA!
Do you have a soother, or could you maybe step out for a minute? It's hard to hear.
Oh! Okay?! My baby's bothering you?
Your baby's bothering the entire class.
Wow!...just wow. Welcome to baby yoga, but please tell your baby to shut the hell up! Real nice!
I'm giving this class **zero** stars on Google and writing a post about how we were treated here today!
WAAA
BYE!
Okay...where were we?

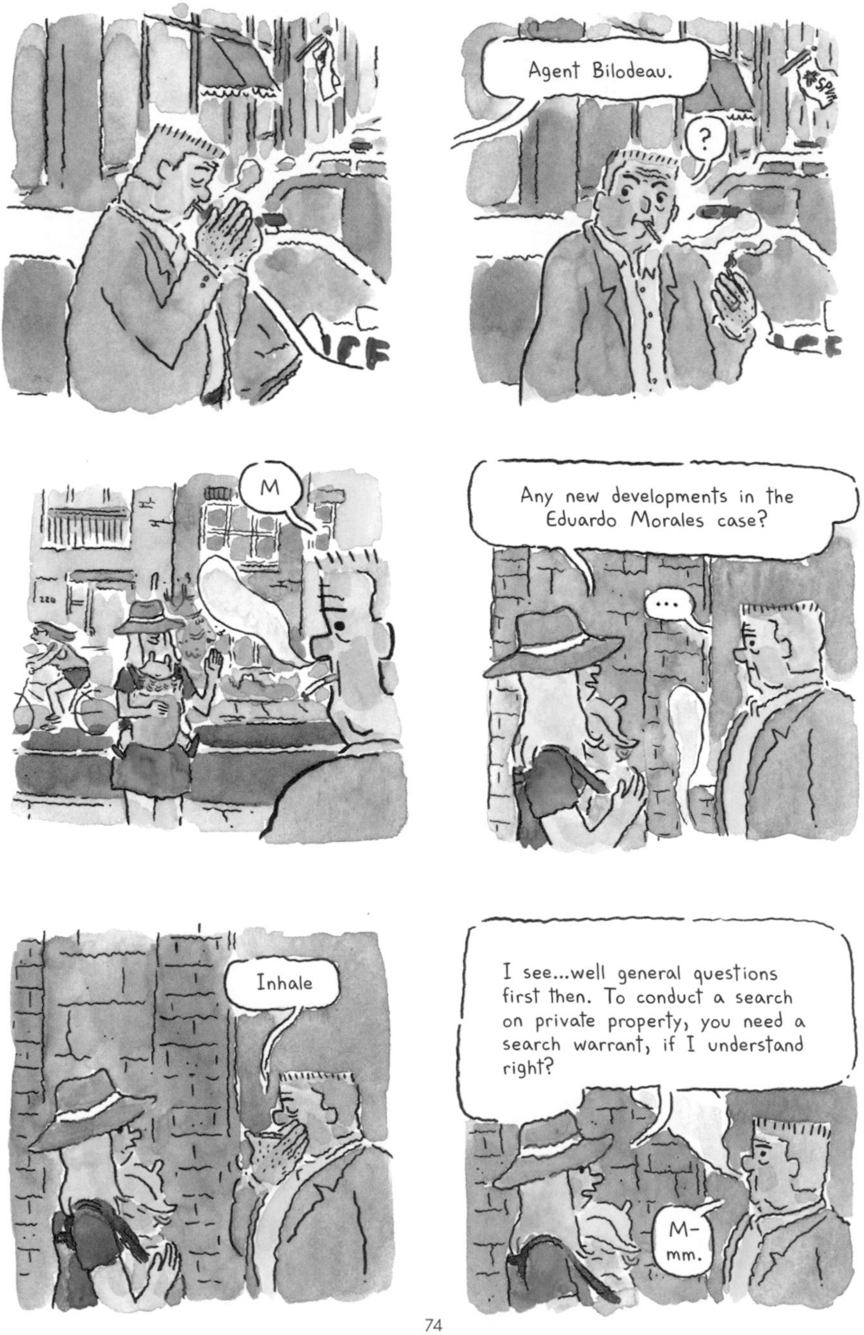
Agent Bilodeau.
?
M
Any new developments in the Eduardo Morales case?
...
Inhale
I see...well general questions first then. To conduct a search on private property, you need a search warrant, if I understand right?
M-mm.

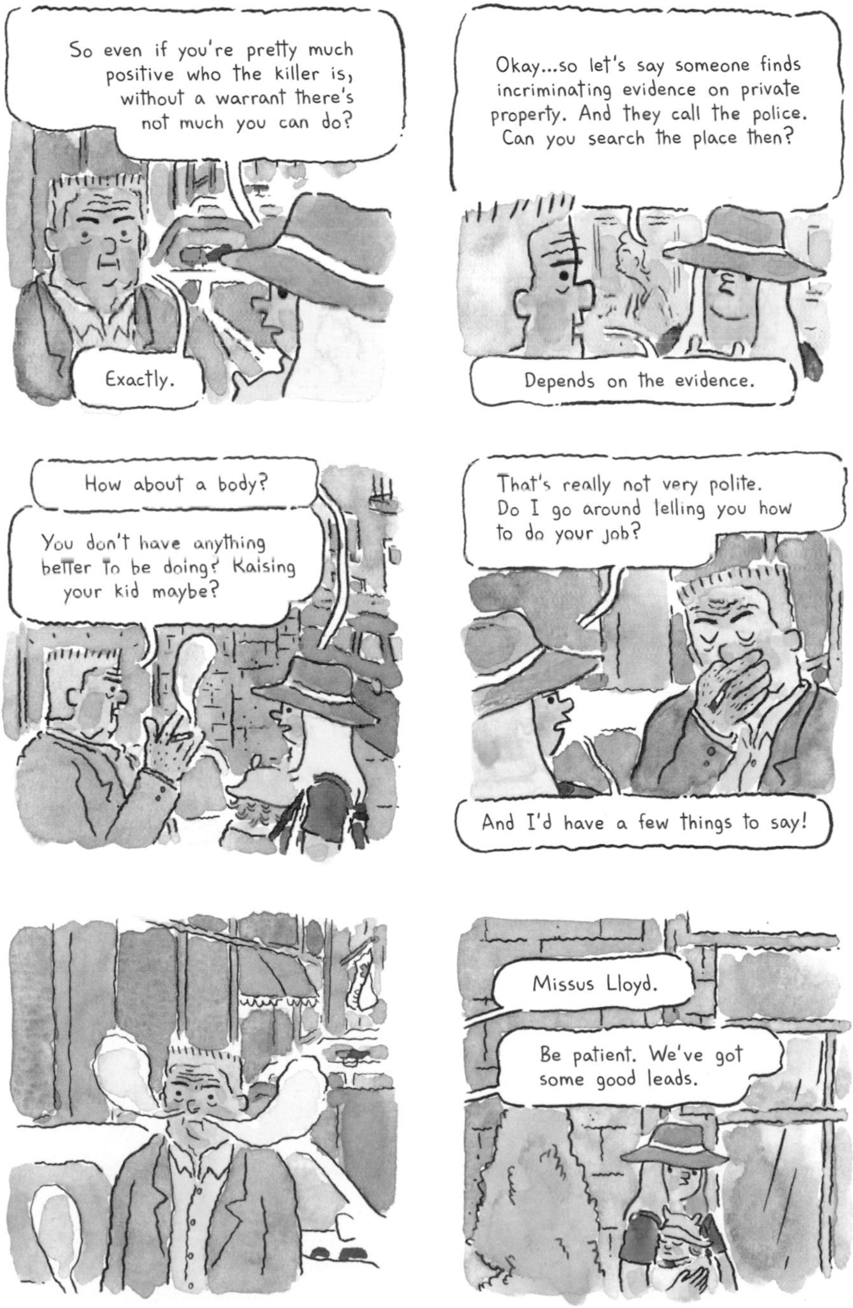
So even if you're pretty much positive who the killer is, without a warrant there's not much you can do?
Exactly.
Okay...so let's say someone finds incriminating evidence on private property. And they call the police. Can you search the place then?
Depends on the evidence.
How about a body?
You don't have anything better to be doing? Kaising your kid maybe?
That's really not very polite. Do I go around telling you how to do your job?
And I'd have a few things to say!
Missus Lloyd.
Be patient. We've got some good leads.

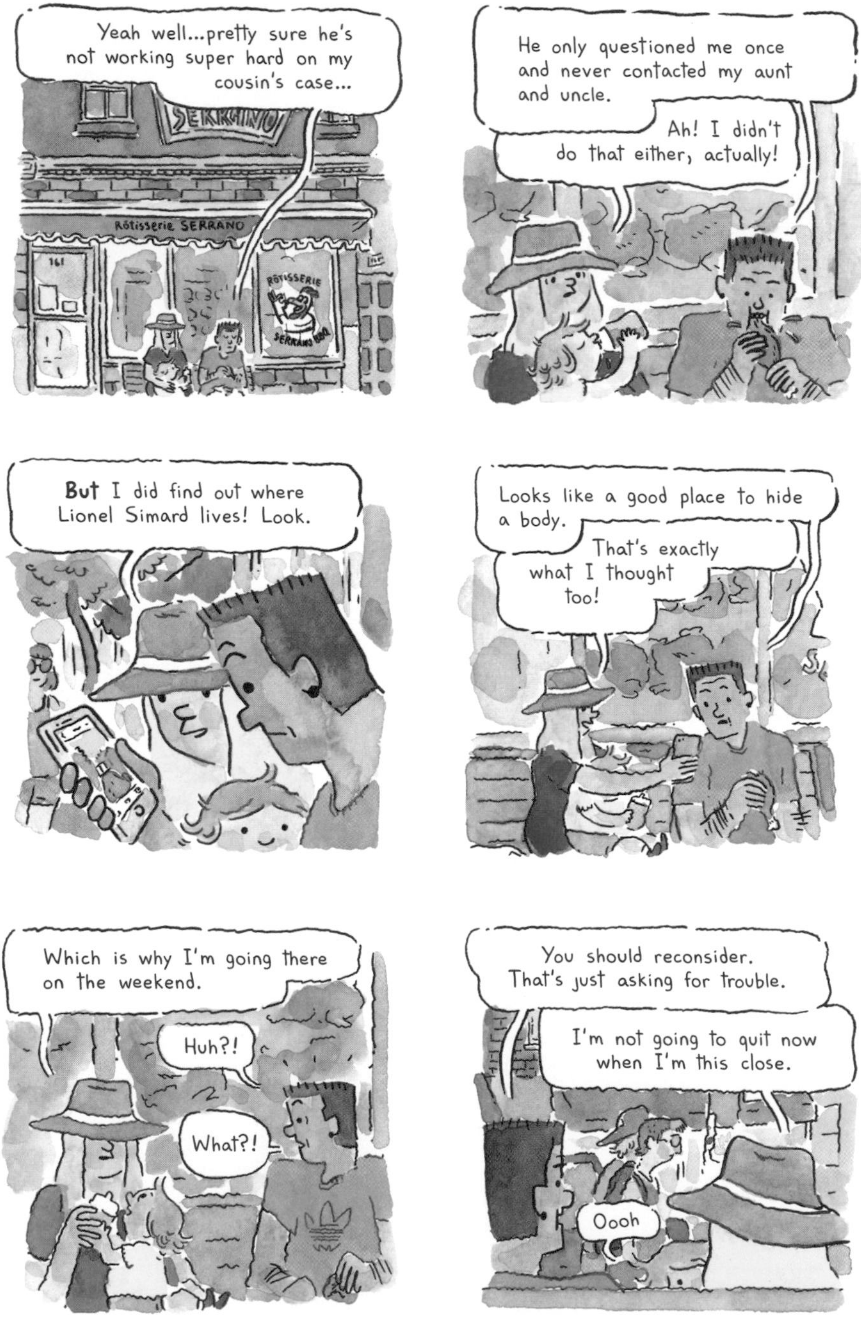

Yeah well...pretty sure he's not working super hard on my cousin's case...
SERRANO
Rôtisserie SERRANO
161
RÔTISSERIE
SERRANO BBQ
He only questioned me once and never contacted my aunt and uncle.
Ah! I didn't do that either, actually!
But I did find out where Lionel Simard lives! Look.
Looks like a good place to hide a body.
That's exactly what I thought too!
Which is why I'm going there on the weekend.
Huh?!
What?!
You should reconsider. That's just asking for trouble.
I'm not going to quit now when I'm this close.
Oooh

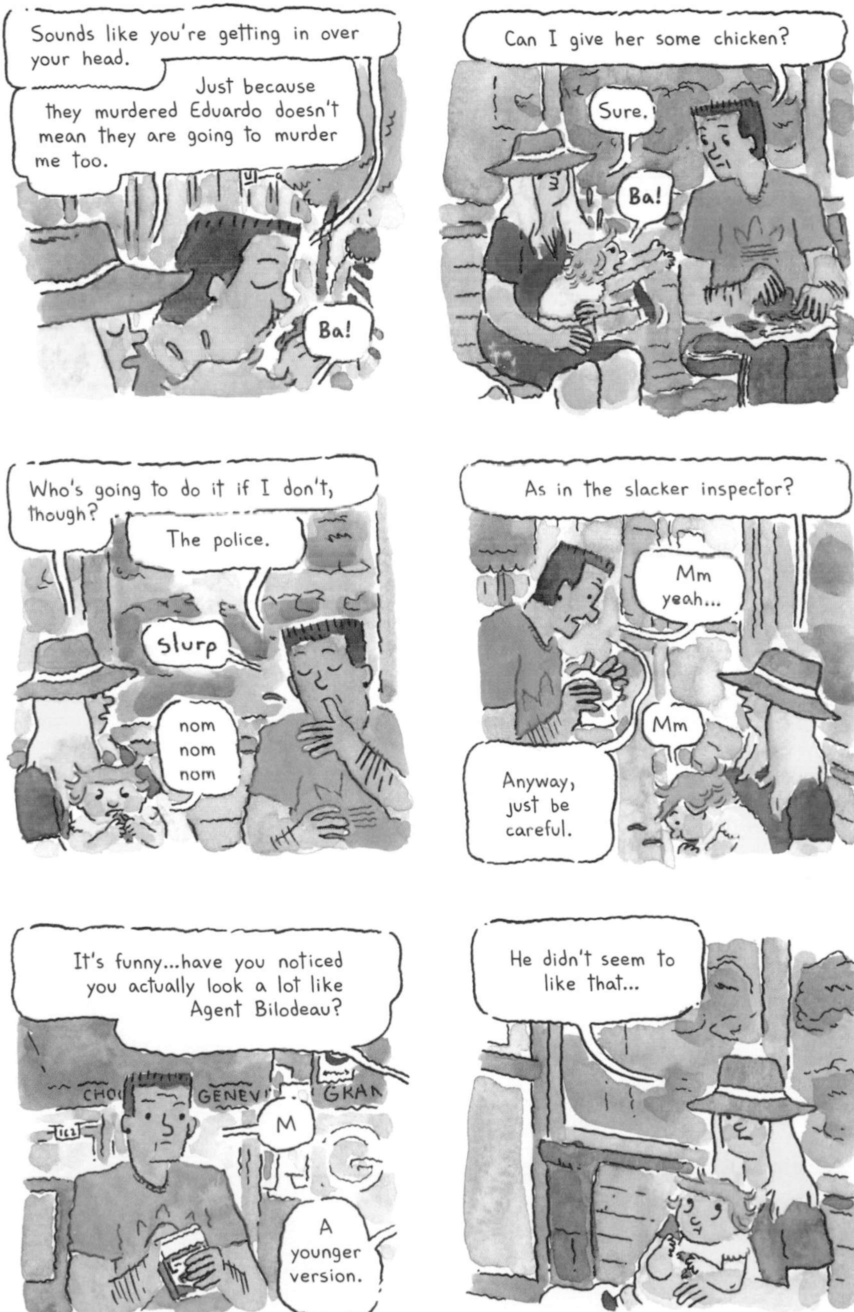
Sounds like you're getting in over your head.
Just because they murdered Eduardo doesn't mean they are going to murder me too.
Ba!
Can I give her some chicken?
Sure.
Ba!
Who's going to do it if I don't, though?
The police.
slurp
nom nom nom
As in the slacker inspector?
Mm yeah...
Mm
Anyway, just be careful.
It's funny...have you noticed you actually look a lot like Agent Bilodeau?
CHO
GENEV
GRAN
M
A younger version.
He didn't seem to like that...

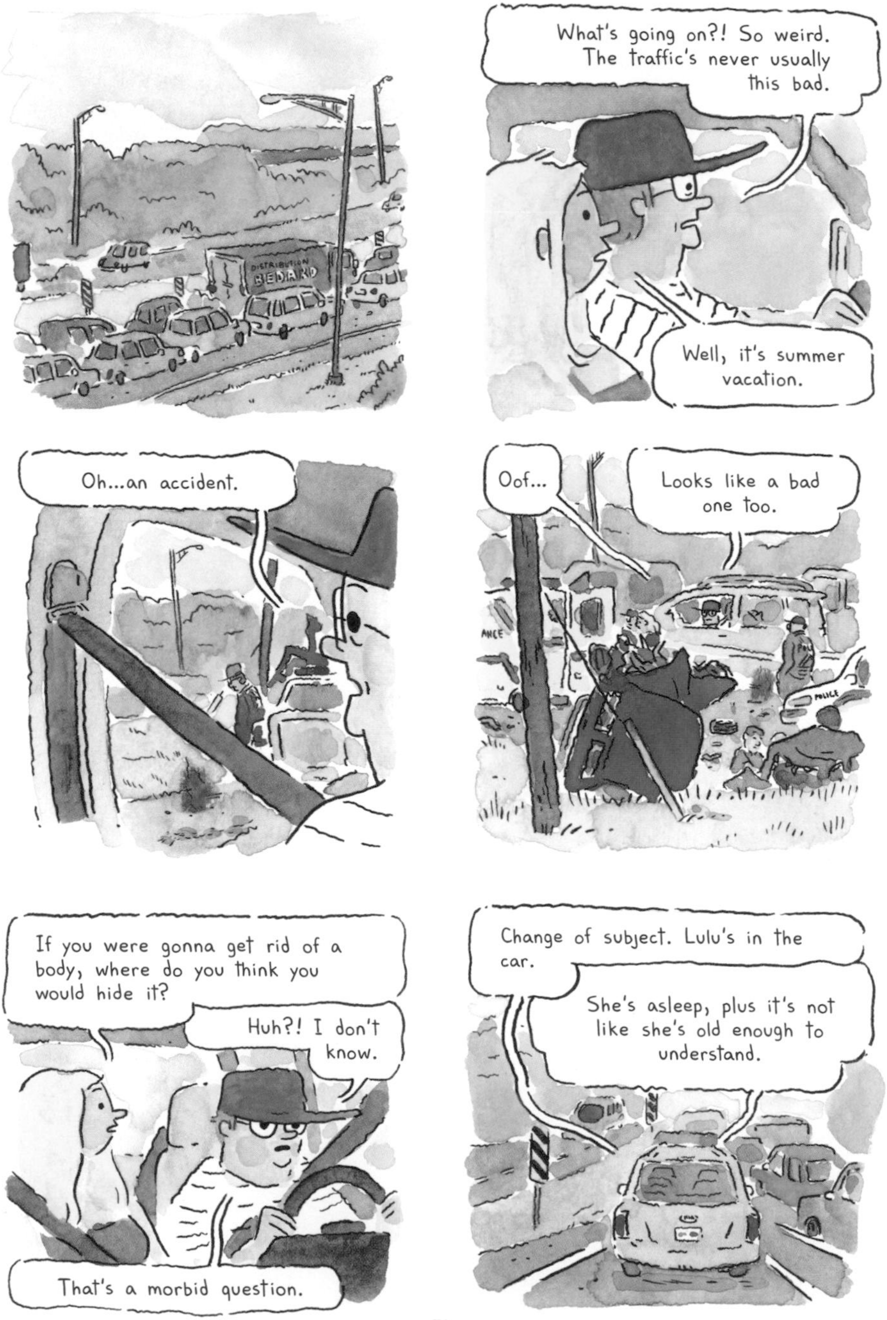
DISTRIBUTION BEDARD
What's going on?! So weird. The traffic's never usually this bad.
Well, it's summer vacation.
Oh...an accident.
Oof...
Looks like a bad one too.
POLICE
If you were gonna get rid of a body, where do you think you would hide it?
Huh?! I don't know.
That's a morbid question.
Change of subject. Lulu's in the car.
She's asleep, plus it's not like she's old enough to understand.

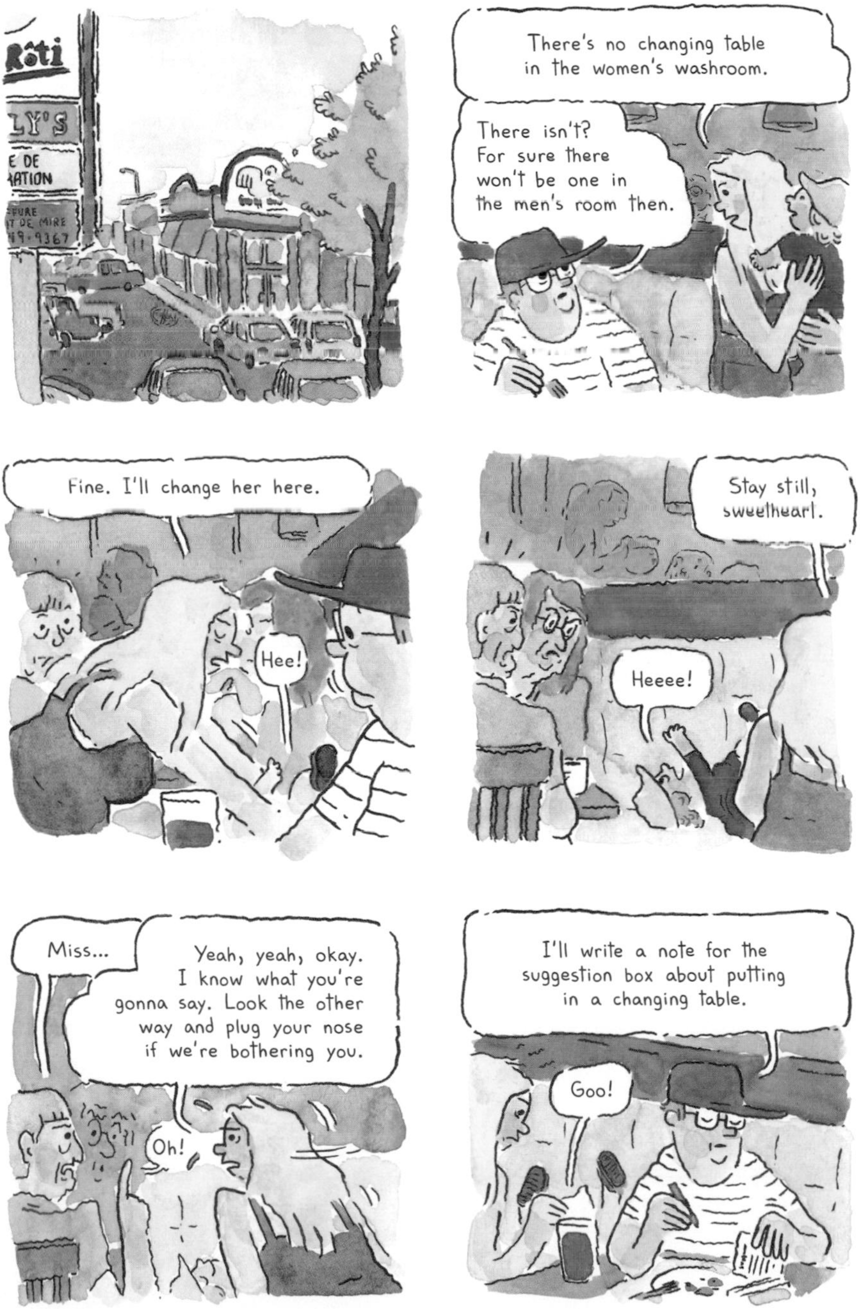
Rôti
LY'S
There's no changing table in the women's washroom.
There isn't? For sure there won't be one in the men's room then.
Fine. I'll change her here.
Hee!
Stay still, sweetheart.
Heeee!
Miss...
Yeah, yeah, okay. I know what you're gonna say. Look the other way and plug your nose if we're bothering you.
Oh!
I'll write a note for the suggestion box about putting in a changing table.
Goo!

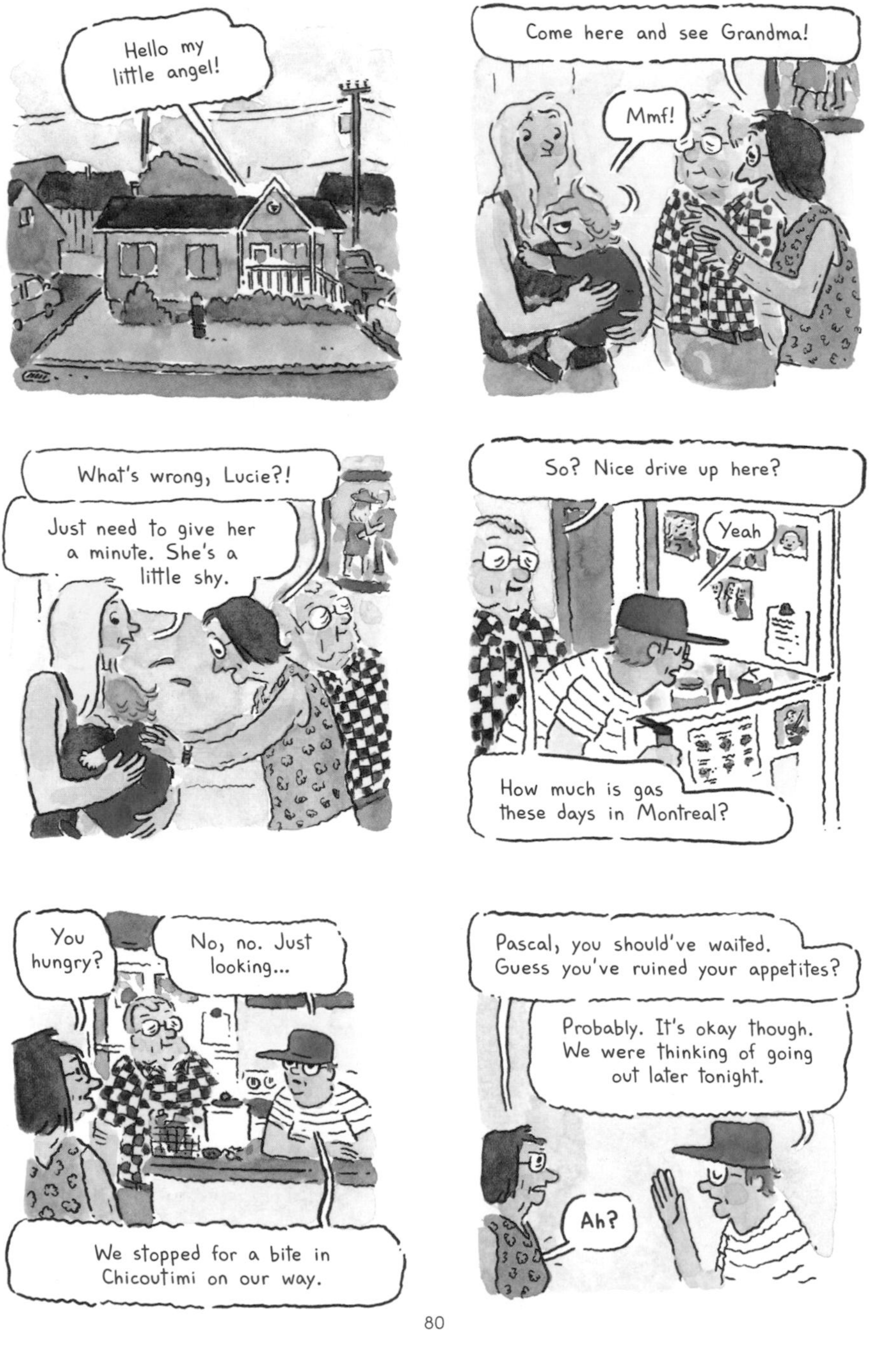
Hello my little angel!
Come here and see Grandma!
Mmf!
What's wrong, Lucie?!
Just need to give her a minute. She's a little shy.
So? Nice drive up here?
Yeah
How much is gas these days in Montreal?
You hungry?
No, no. Just looking...
We stopped for a bite in Chicoutimi on our way.
Pascal, you should've waited. Guess you've ruined your appetites?
Probably. It's okay though. We were thinking of going out later tonight.
Ah?

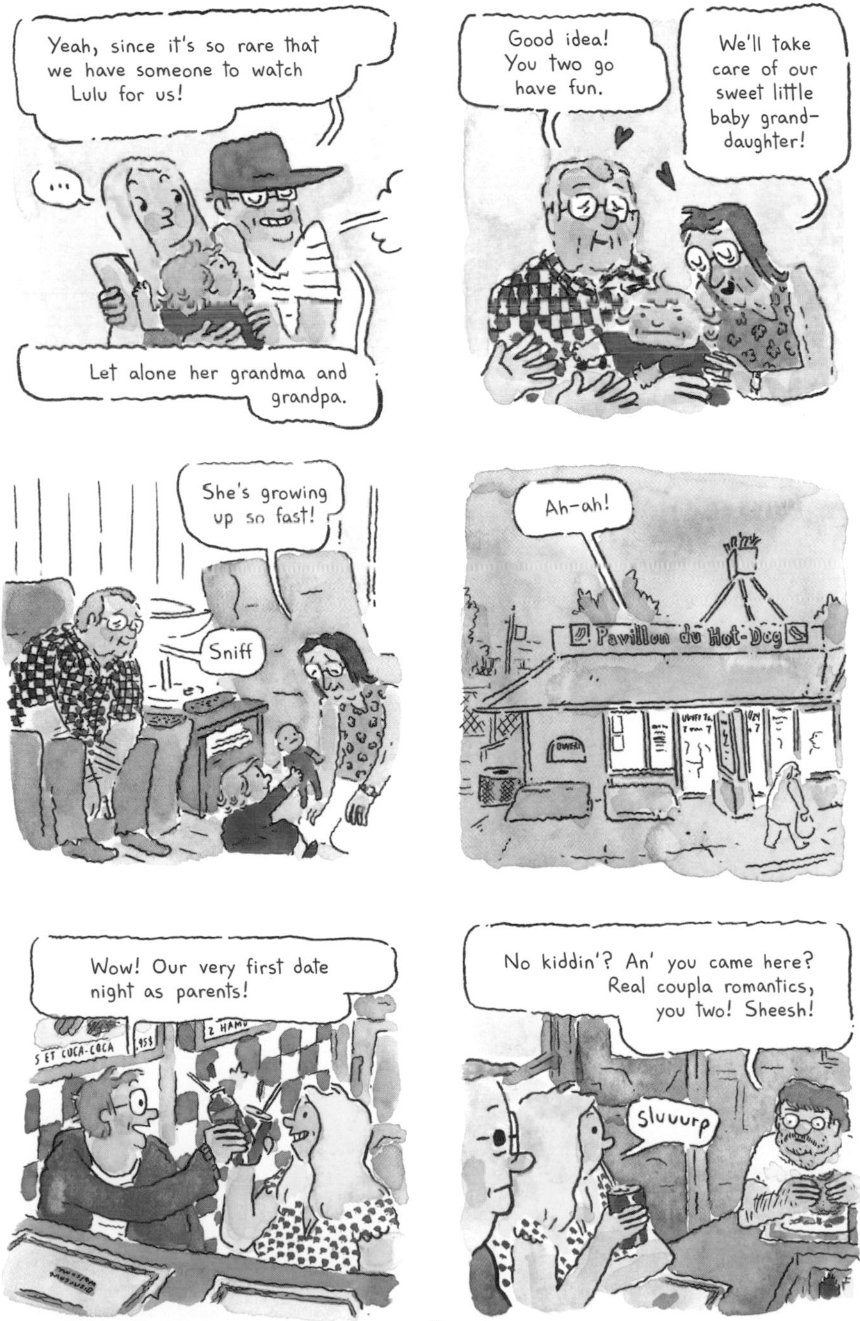
Yeah, since it's so rare that we have someone to watch Lulu for us!
...
Let alone her grandma and grandpa.
Good idea! You two go have fun.
We'll take care of our sweet little baby grand-daughter!
She's growing up so fast!
Sniff
Ah-ah!
Pavillon du Hot-Dog
Wow! Our very first date night as parents!
No kiddin'? An' you came here? Real coupla romantics, you two! Sheesh!
Sluuurp

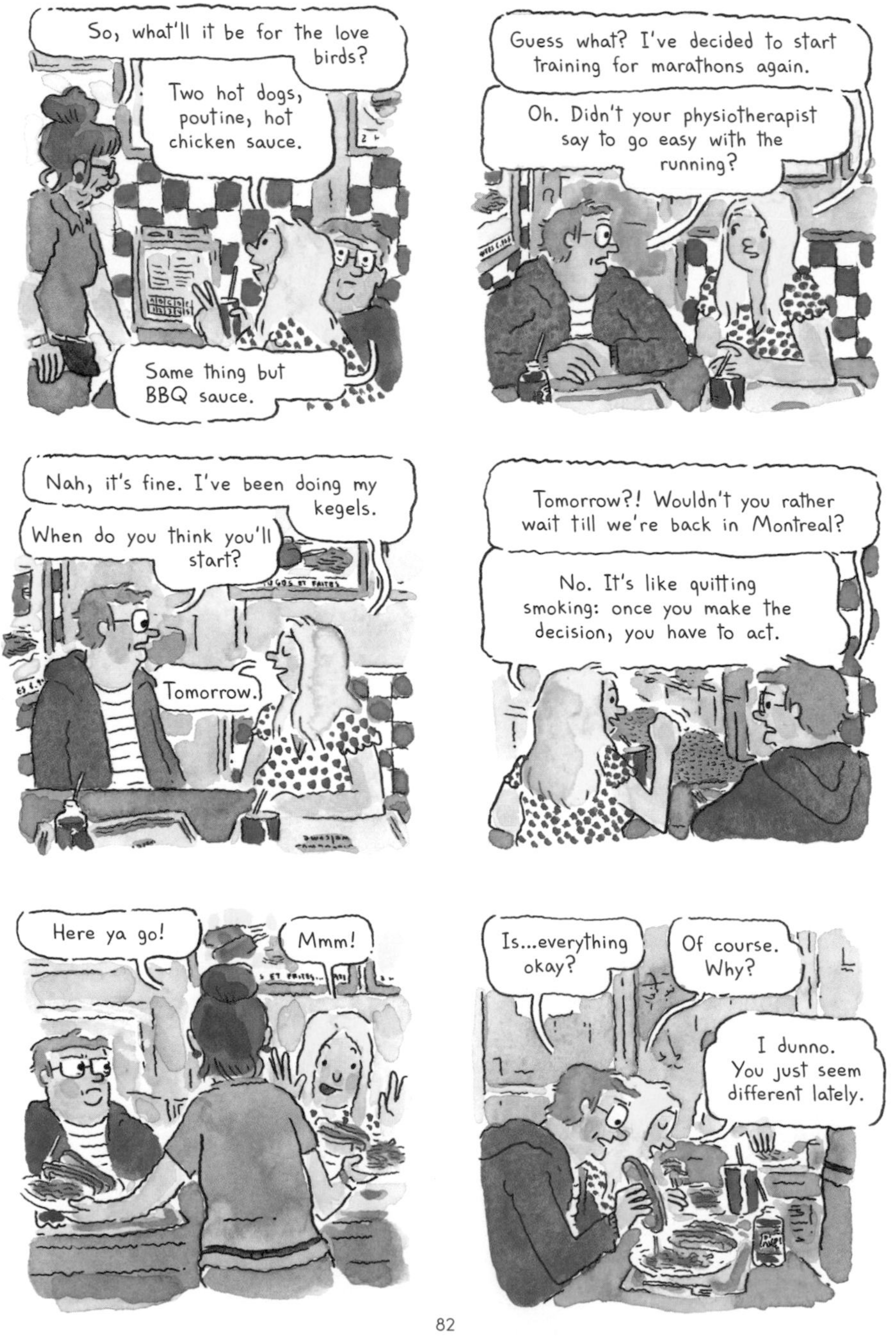
So, what'll it be for the love birds?
Two hot dogs, poutine, hot chicken sauce.
Same thing but BBQ sauce.
Guess what? I've decided to start training for marathons again.
Oh. Didn't your physiotherapist say to go easy with the running?
Nah, it's fine. I've been doing my kegels.
When do you think you'll start?
Tomorrow.
Tomorrow?! Wouldn't you rather wait till we're back in Montreal?
No. It's like quitting smoking: once you make the decision, you have to act.
Here ya go!
Mmm!
Is...everything okay?
Of course. Why?
I dunno. You just seem different lately.

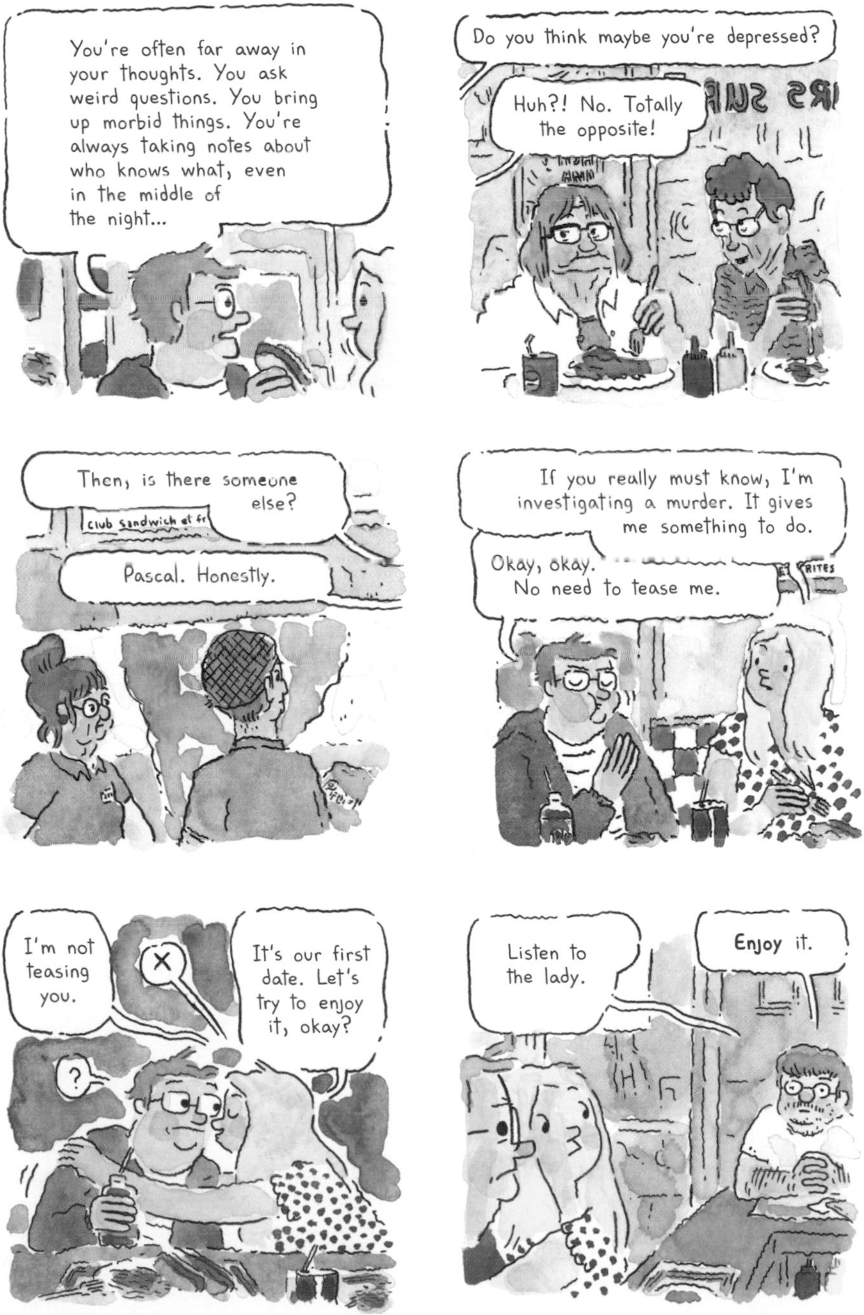
You're often far away in your thoughts. You ask weird questions. You bring up morbid things. You're always taking notes about who knows what, even in the middle of the night...
Do you think maybe you're depressed?
Huh?! No. Totally the opposite!
Then, is there someone else?
club sandwich
Pascal. Honestly.
If you really must know, I'm investigating a murder. It gives me something to do.
Okay, okay. No need to tease me.
RITES
I'm not teasing you.
It's our first date. Let's try to enjoy it, okay?
?
Listen to the lady.
Enjoy it.

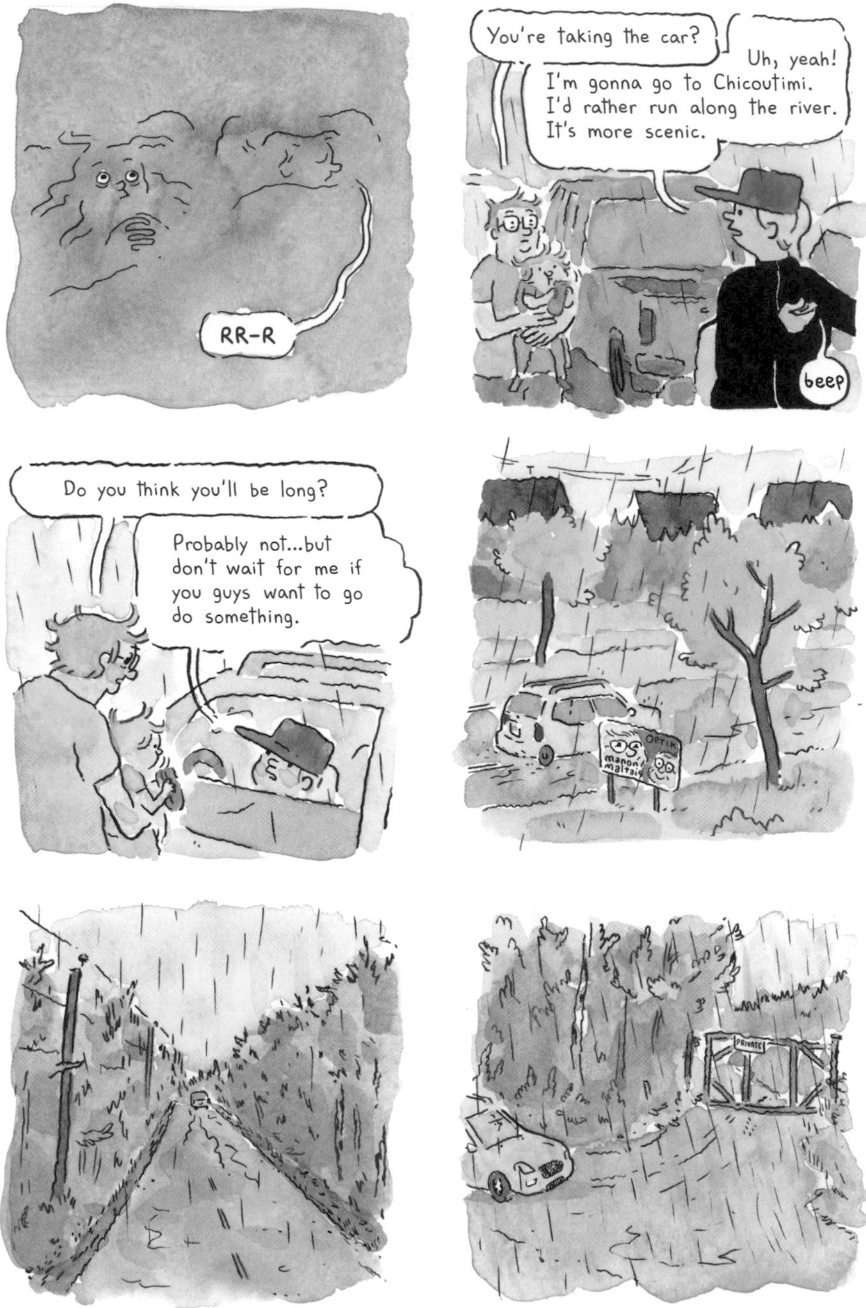
RR-R
You're taking the car?
Uh, yeah! I'm gonna go to Chicoutimi. I'd rather run along the river. It's more scenic.
beep
Do you think you'll be long?
Probably not...but don't wait for me if you guys want to go do something.
OPTIK
manon maltais
PRIVATE

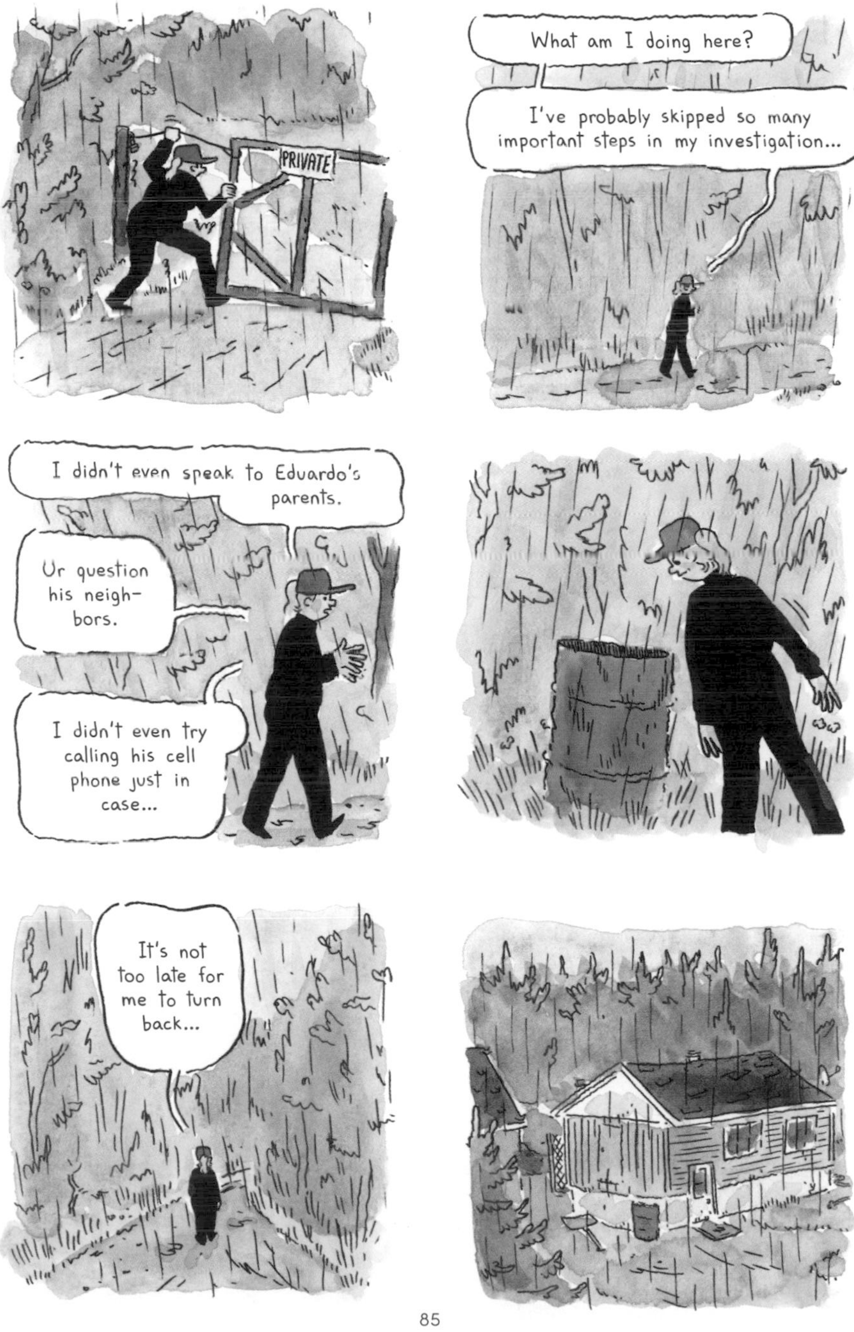
PRIVATE
What am I doing here?
I've probably skipped so many important steps in my investigation...
I didn't even speak to Eduardo's parents.
Or question his neighbors.
I didn't even try calling his cell phone just in case...
It's not too late for me to turn back...

Creee

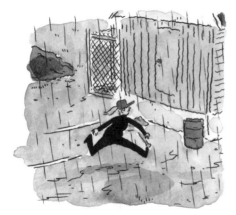

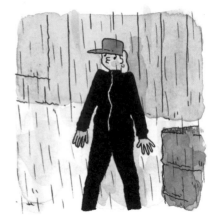

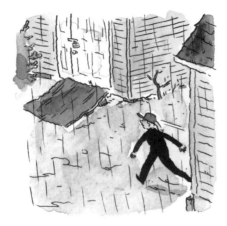

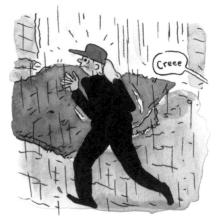

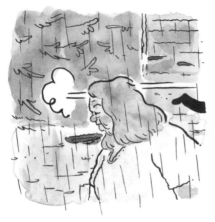

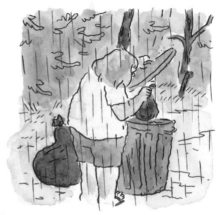

Cough
Cough
clonk
...

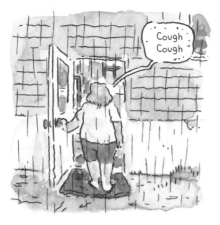

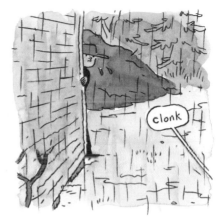

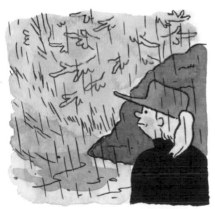

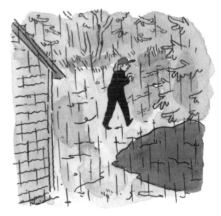

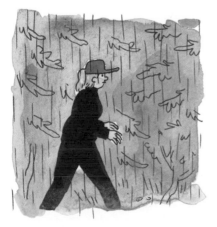

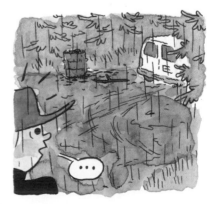

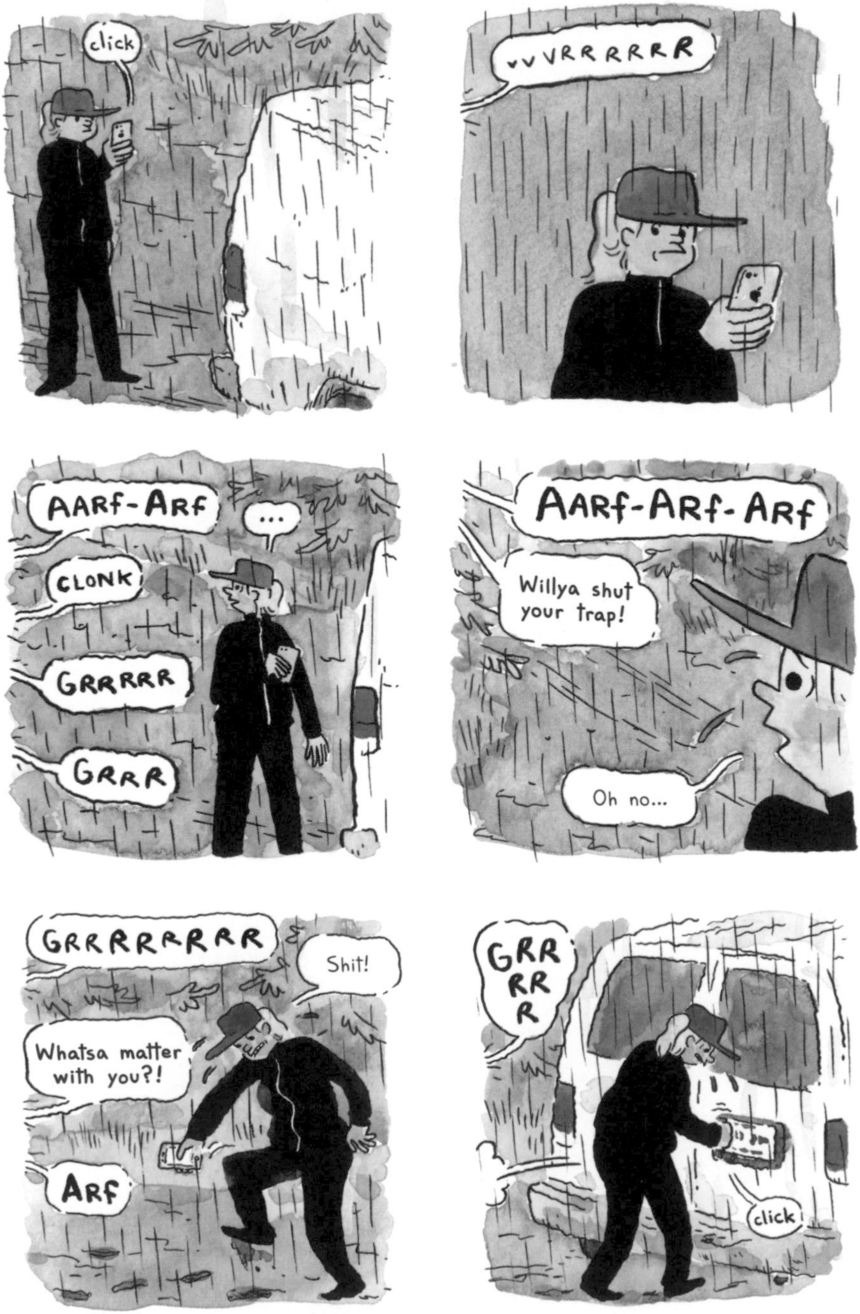
click
vvVRRRRRR
AARf-ARf
...
CLONK
GRRRRR
GRRR
AARf-ARf-ARf
Willya shut your trap!
Oh no...
GRRRRRRRR
Shit!
Whatsa matter with you?!
Arf
GRR RR R
click

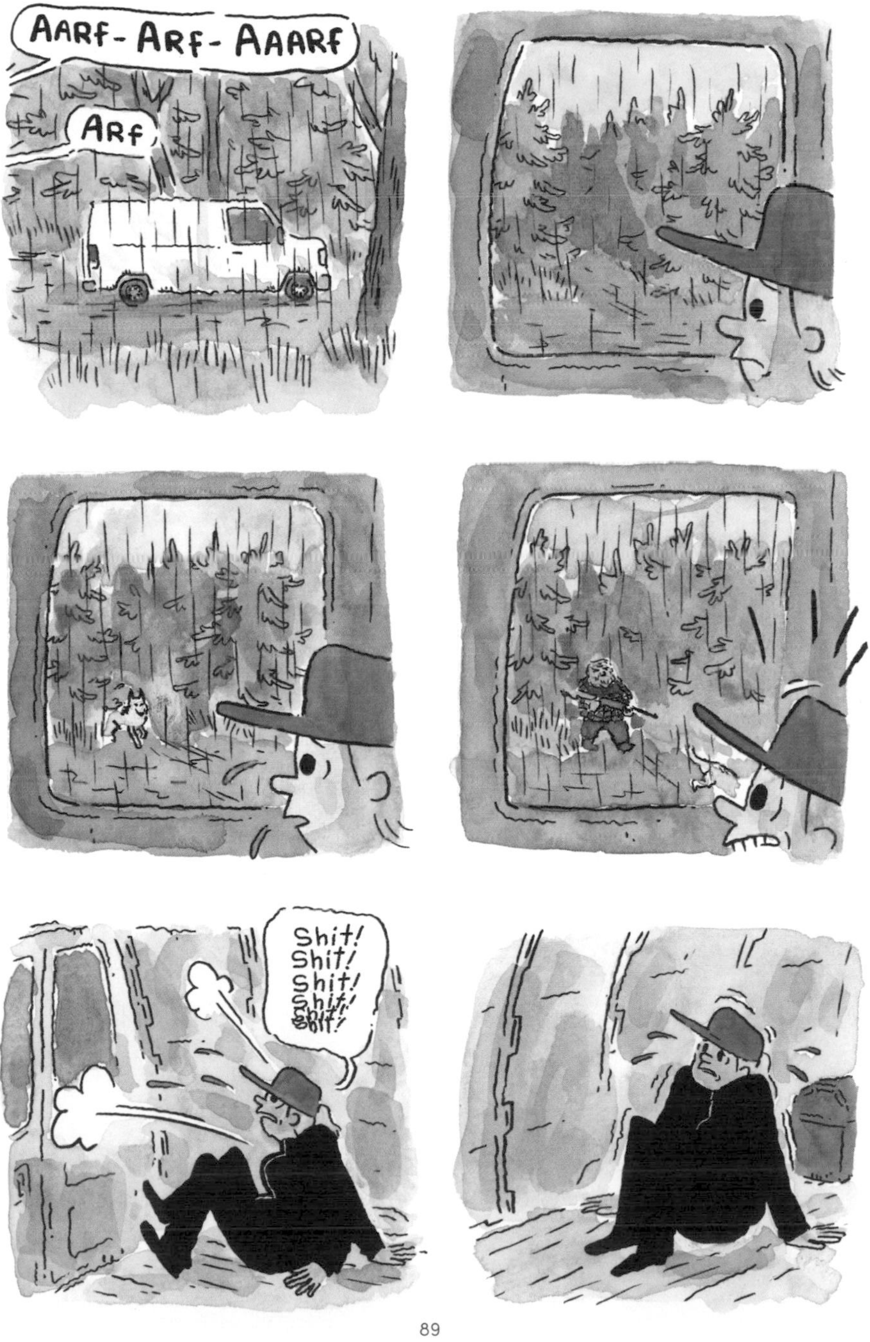
AARF-ARF-AAARF
ARF
Shit!
Shit!
Shit!
Shit!
Shit!

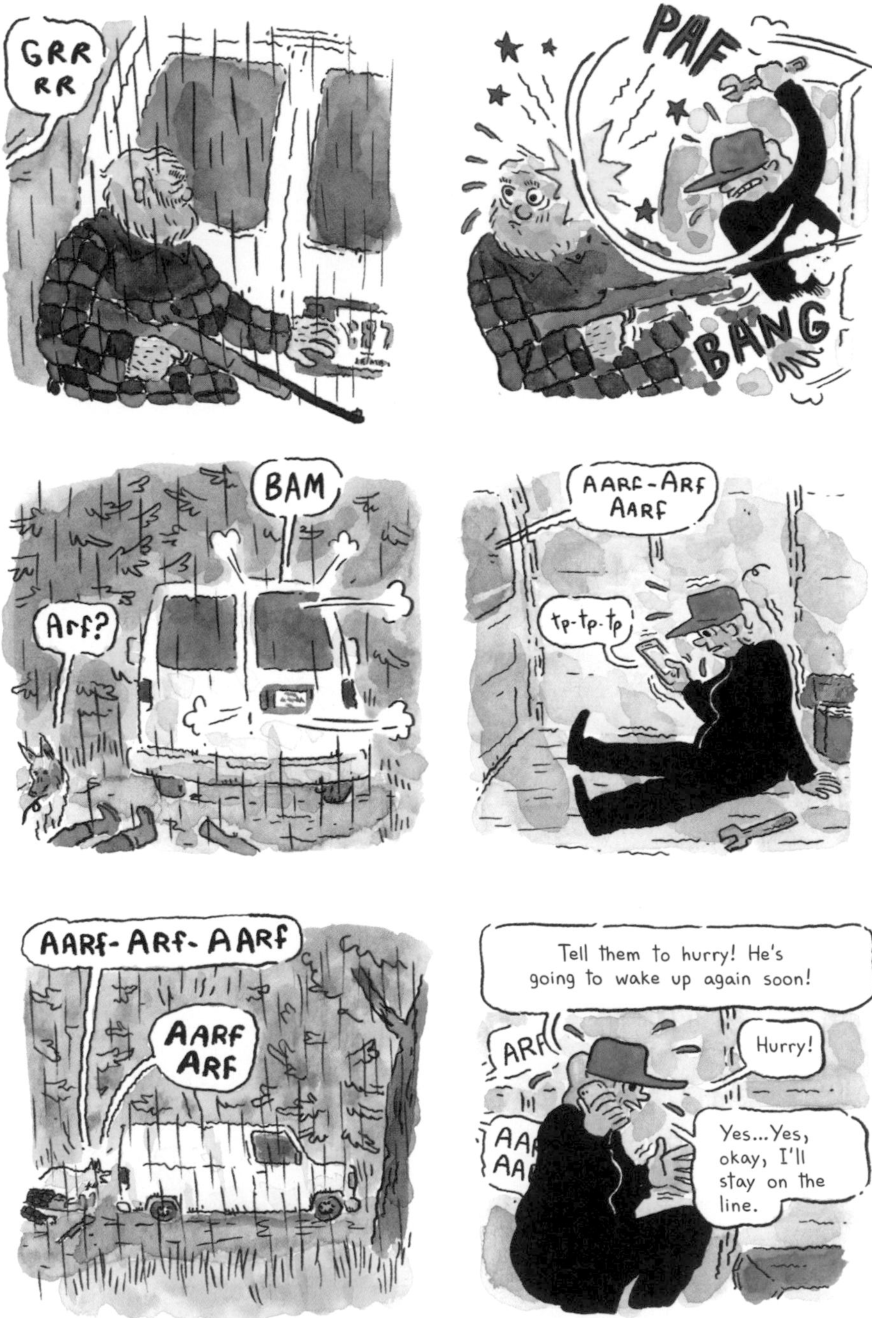
GRR RR
PAF
BANG
BAM
Arf?
AARF-ARF AARF
tp-tp-tp
AARF-ARF-AARF
AARF ARF
Tell them to hurry! He's going to wake up again soon!
Hurry!
Yes...Yes, okay, I'll stay on the line.

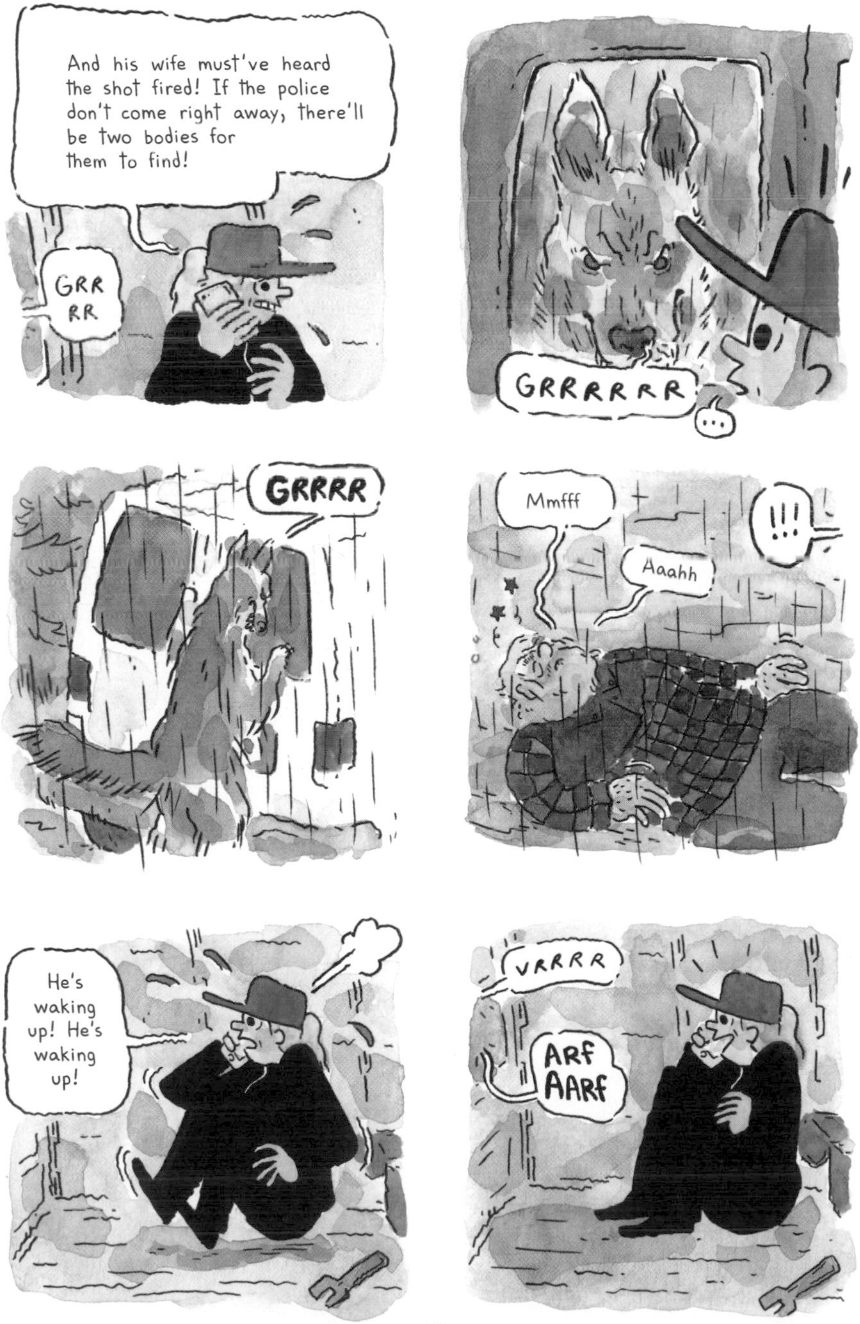
And his wife must've heard the shot fired! If the police don't come right away, there'll be two bodies for them to find!
GRR RR
GRRRRRR
...
GRRRR
Mmfff
!!!
Aaahh
He's waking up! He's waking up!
VRRRR
ARF AARF

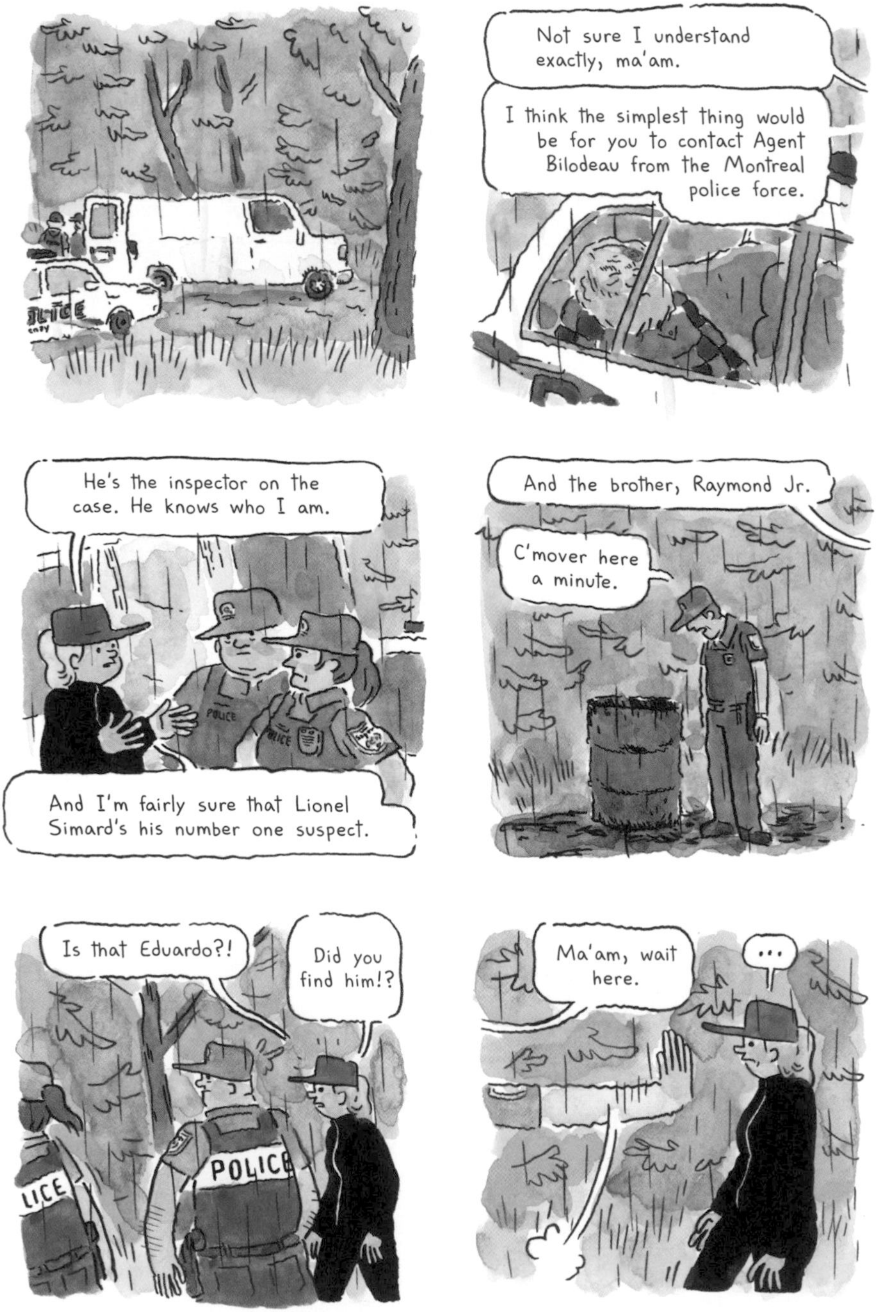

POLICE
Not sure I understand exactly, ma'am.
I think the simplest thing would be for you to contact Agent Bilodeau from the Montreal police force.
He's the inspector on the case. He knows who I am.
POLICE
POLICE
And I'm fairly sure that Lionel Simard's his number one suspect.
And the brother, Raymond Jr.
C'mover here a minute.
Is that Eduardo?!
Did you find him!?
LICE
POLICE
Ma'am, wait here.
...

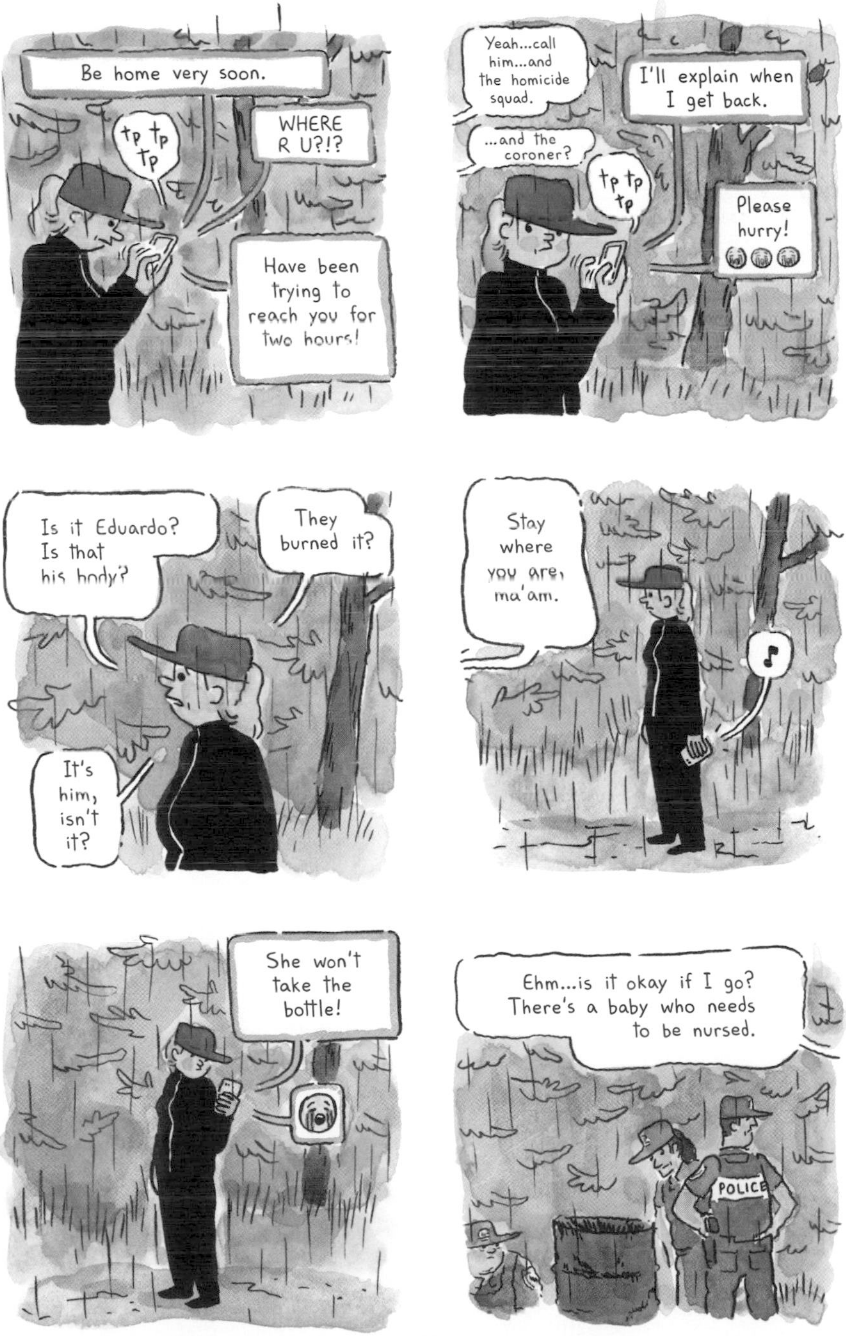
Be home very soon.
tp tp tp
WHERE R U?!?
Have been trying to reach you for two hours!
Yeah...call him...and the homicide squad.
I'll explain when I get back.
...and the coroner?
tp tp tp
Please hurry!
Is it Eduardo? Is that his body?
They burned it?
It's him, isn't it?
Stay where you are, ma'am.
She won't take the bottle!
Ehm...is it okay if I go? There's a baby who needs to be nursed.
POLICE

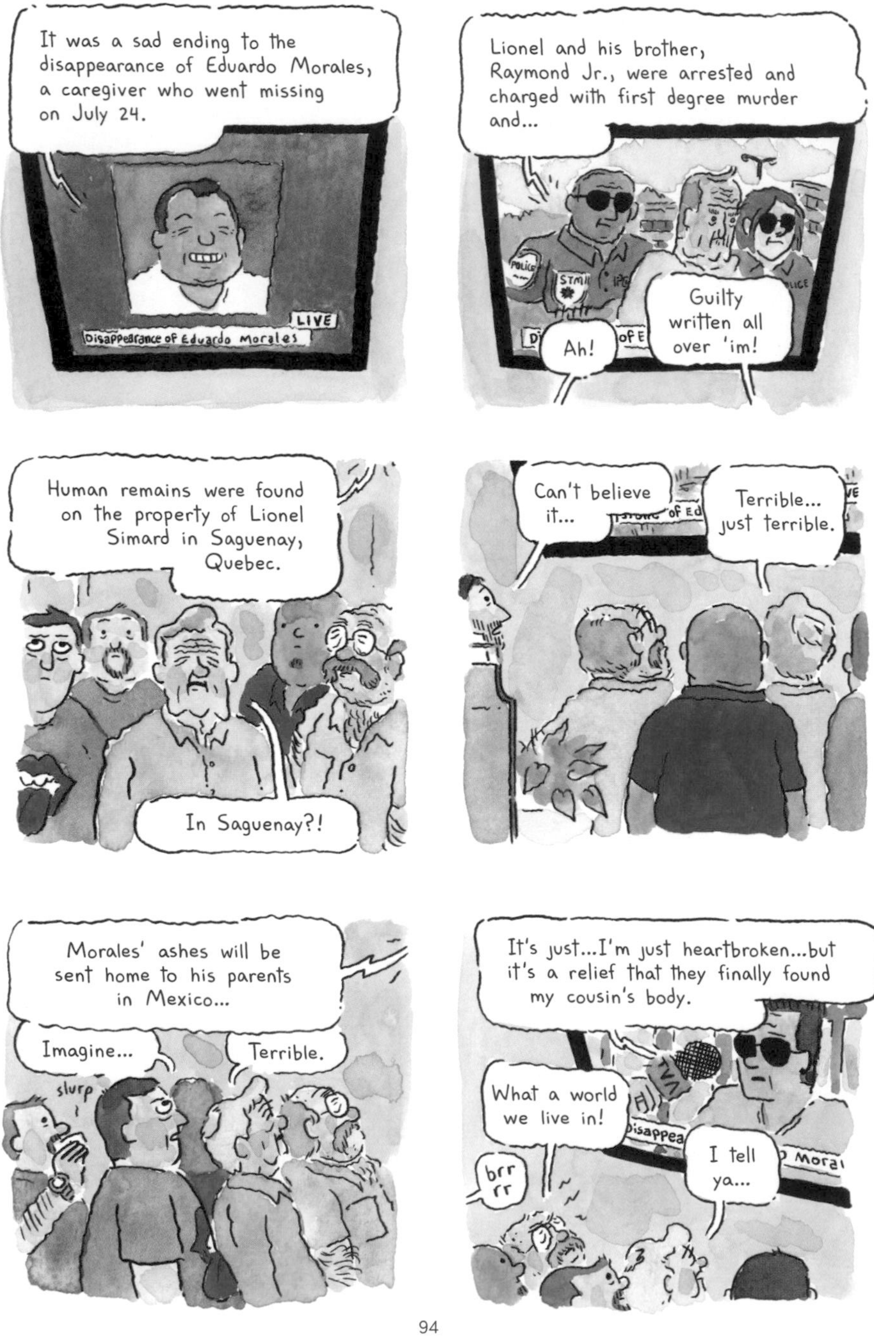
It was a sad ending to the disappearance of Eduardo Morales, a caregiver who went missing on July 24.
LIVE
Disappearance of Eduardo Morales
Lionel and his brother, Raymond Jr., were arrested and charged with first degree murder and...
Ah!
Guilty written all over 'im!
Human remains were found on the property of Lionel Simard in Saguenay, Quebec.
In Saguenay?!
Can't believe it...
Terrible... just terrible.
Morales' ashes will be sent home to his parents in Mexico...
Imagine...
Terrible.
slurp
It's just...I'm just heartbroken...but it's a relief that they finally found my cousin's body.
What a world we live in!
brr rr
I tell ya...

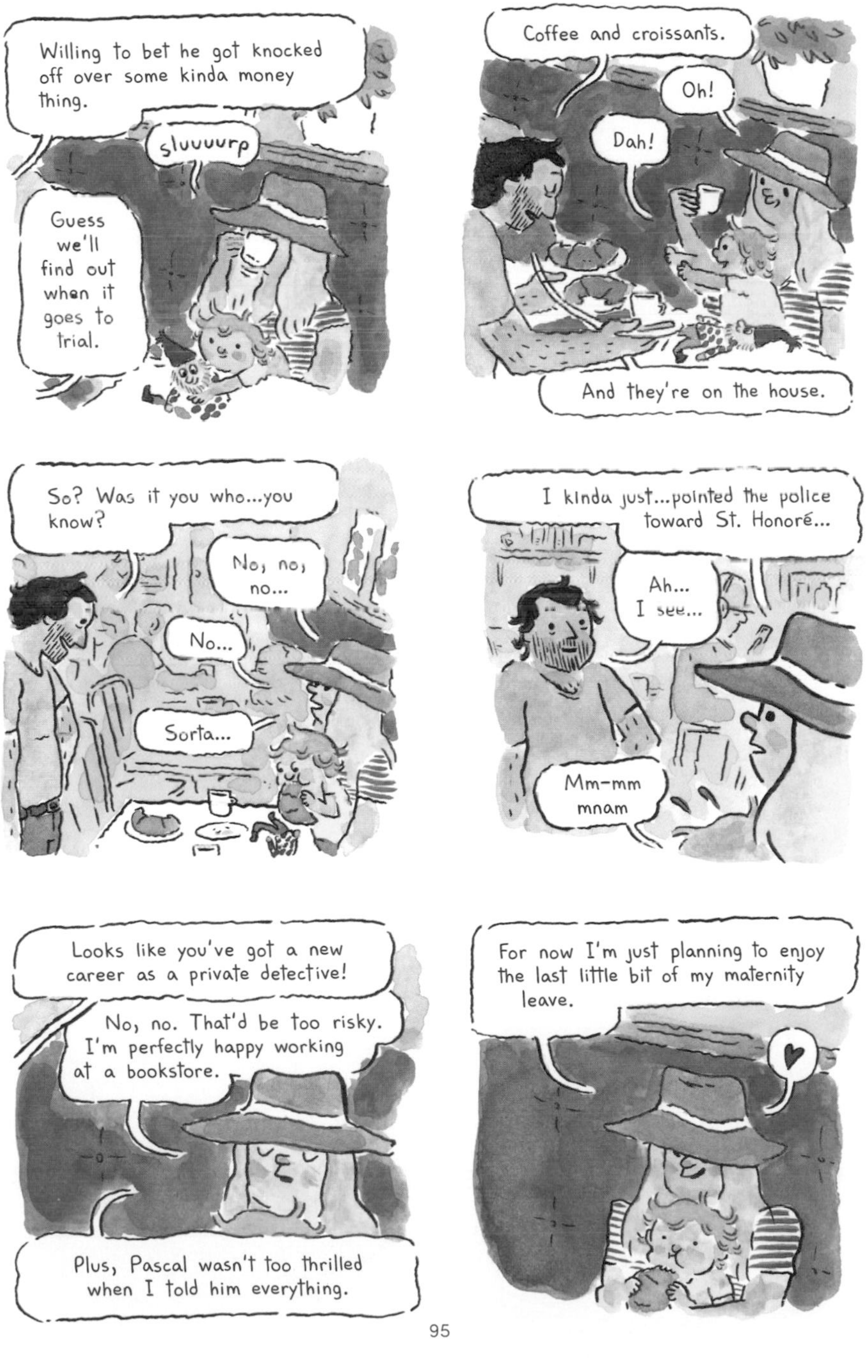
Willing to bet he got knocked off over some kinda money thing.
sluuuurp
Guess we'll find out when it goes to trial.
Coffee and croissants.
Oh!
Dah!
And they're on the house.
So? Was it you who...you know?
No, no, no...
No...
Sorta...
I kinda just...pointed the police toward St. Honoré...
Ah... I see...
Mm-mm mnam
Looks like you've got a new career as a private detective!
No, no. That'd be too risky. I'm perfectly happy working at a bookstore.
Plus, Pascal wasn't too thrilled when I told him everything.
For now I'm just planning to enjoy the last little bit of my maternity leave.

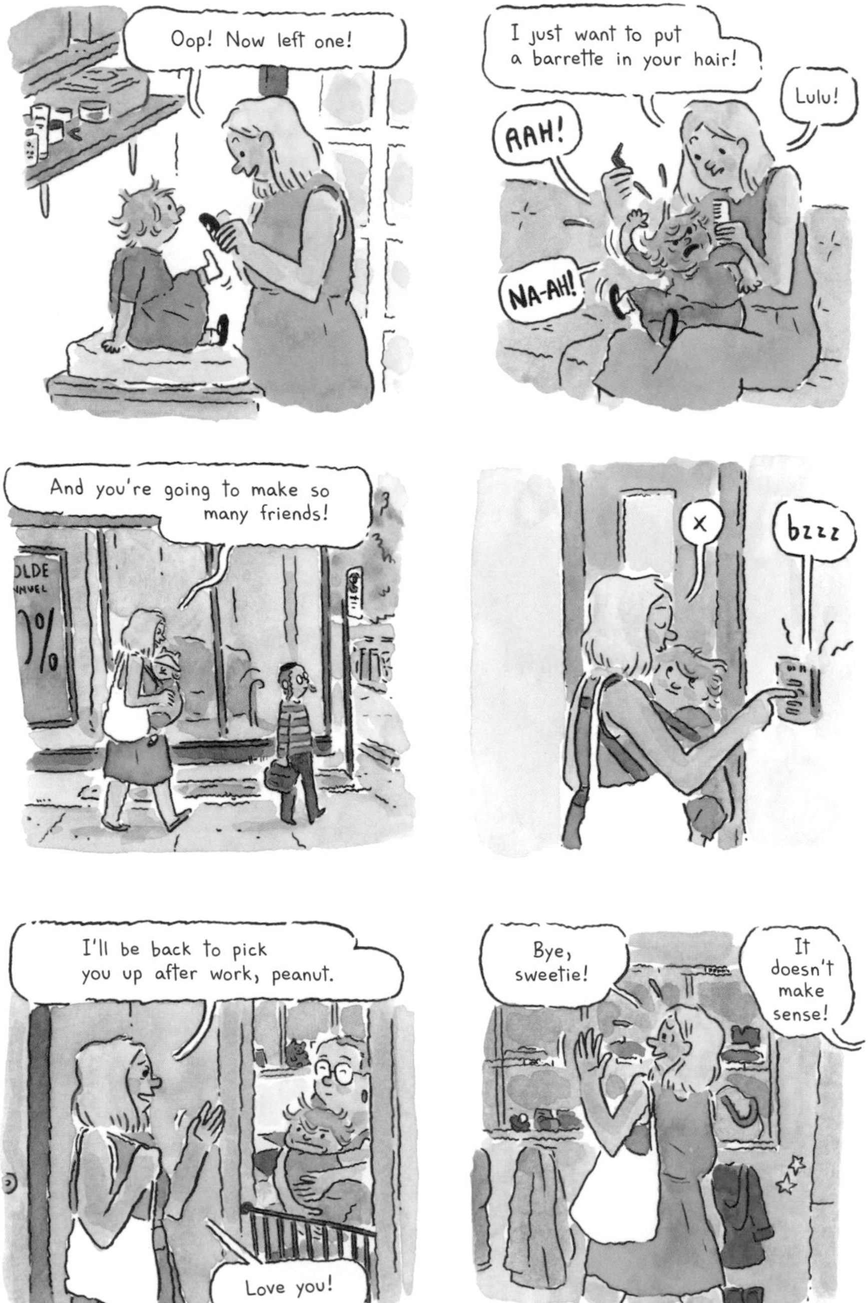

Oop! Now left one!
I just want to put a barrette in your hair!
Lulu!
AAH!
NA-AH!
And you're going to make so many friends!
x
bzzz
I'll be back to pick you up after work, peanut.
Love you!
Bye, sweetie!
It doesn't make sense!

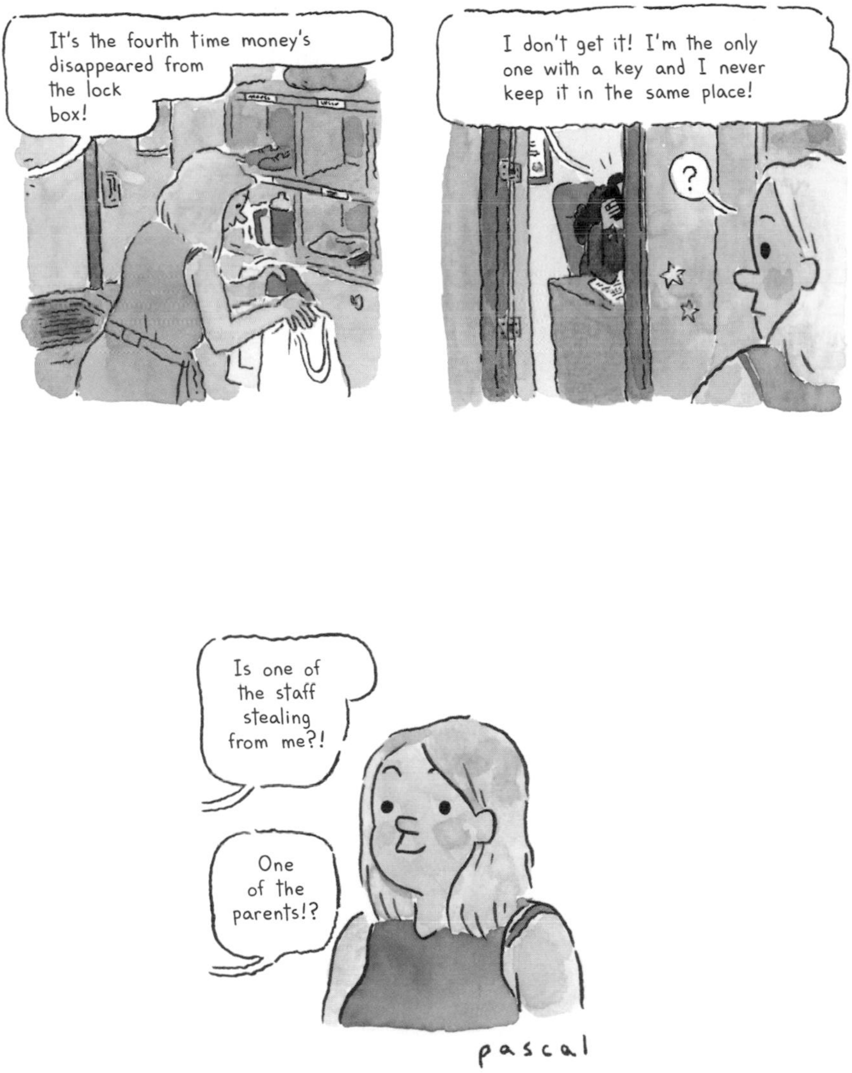
It's the fourth time money's disappeared from the lock box!
I don't get it! I'm the only one with a key and I never keep it in the same place!
?
Is one of the staff stealing from me?!
One of the parents!?
pascal

For Rebecca

Pascal Girard was born in Jonquière, QC, in 1981. He is a part-time cartoonist and part-time social worker. He is the award-winning author of *Nicolas*, *Bigfoot*, *Reunion*, and *Petty Theft*. He lives in Montréal with his family.